*Women Philosophers
of the
Early Modern Period*

Women Philosophers of the Early Modern Period

✧ EDITED, WITH INTRODUCTION, BY
Margaret Atherton

Hackett Publishing Company
Indianapolis/Cambridge

20   19   18   17   5   6   7   8   9   10

For further information, please adress

Hackett Publishing Company, Inc.
P.O. Box 44937
Indianapolis, Indiana 46244-0937

www.hackettpublishing.com

Cover and text design by Harrison Shaffer

Production coordination: Elizabeth Shaw Editorial and Publishing
Services, Tucson, Arizona

Library of Congress Cataloging-in-Publication Data

Women philosophers of the early modern period/edited, with
    introduction, by Margaret Atherton.
            p.   cm.
        Includes bibliographical references.
        ISBN 0-87220-260-7 (cloth).   ISBN 0-87220-259-3 (pbk.)
        1. Philosophy.   2. Women philosophers.   3. Philosophy,
    Modern—17th century.   4. Philosophy, Modern—18th century.
    I. Atherton, Margaret.
    B801.W65   1994
    190'.82—dc20   94-27004
                                                                    CIP

ISBN-13: 978-0-87220-260-3 (cloth)
ISBN-13: 978-0-87220-259-7 (pbk.)

To my mother
Barbara B. Atherton
For her example
and her encouragement
of educated women

Contents

Acknowledgments

WORK ON THIS ANTHOLOGY was supported in part by a Fellowship from the Institute of the Humanities at the University of Wisconsin at Madison. I owe a special debt to Kathleen Cook for suggesting that I put together an anthology of this sort and for the thoughtful discussions I have had with her about the history of women in philosophy over many years. I am grateful to Kenneth Winkler, Hackett's reader, and, as always, to Robert Schwartz, for advice on an earlier draft. I want to thank Margo Anderson and Stacey Oliker for listening, and Margo for years of encouragement.

I also owe a debt to all those who have helped recover and preserve the work of women philosophers of the early modern period. Although they are much too numerous for me to mention all of them, I feel I owe a special debt to Hilda Smith and Katharine Rogers for making available knowledge of the vast number of women writers, including philosophers, of the seventeenth and eighteenth centuries, and for getting me started in this work.

Several philosophers have performed extraordinarily valuable service in bringing to the fore the existence and nature of the work of women philosophers throughout history. I have been particularly aided by the work of Mary Ellen Waithe, Linda McAlister and Eileen O'Neill. I am grateful to O'Neill for providing me with a copy of the syllabus for her course in women philosophers of the early modern period.

Among others, Ruth Perry, Martha Bolton, and Sarah Hutton have provided models of scholarship on women philosophers. I also want to mention the work of Elizabeth Godfrey and Florence Smith who, in the early days of this century, recovered and wrote about the work of Princess Elisabeth and Mary Astell, respectively. It is my hope that, through my work and that of the others in this area, women philosophers will no longer need to be recovered.

Introduction

THE SEVENTEENTH AND EIGHTEENTH centuries—the early modern period—are noted for their remarkably high level of philosophical activity. What has been obscured, however, is the fact that women as well as men wrote and published philosophy during that time. Indeed, the standard course in the history of early modern philosophy that focuses on the canonical writers of the period perpetuates an erroneous impression that, at the time, only men were philosophers. Redressing the balance has been very difficult, because the majority of works by women have not been republished since they were originally written and they can be found only in a few research libraries or on microfilm. The purpose of this anthology is to make available to interested readers a selection from the writings of women philosophers of the period, and to make it possible to incorporate a study of their writings into history of modern philosophy courses.

The seven women whose work is included here were, in some ways, atypical of their female contemporaries. This was not a period in which women had a great deal of access to education. Any education girls received took place at home, and the sixteenth-century tradition of giving daughters of the aristocracy an extensive education was dying out. Of the women included here, only Princess Elisabeth of Bohemia seems to have been the beneficiary of the earlier custom of providing an education for young women at home that went beyond basic accomplishments. The other women included in this anthology were largely self-educated, although some were able to take advantage of favorable conditions at home, such as fathers or brothers who supported their education. Only rarely was a woman able to acquire the training necessary to enter into philosophical discussion, whose full participation required a knowledge of Latin and French or English.

It also seems that each of these women felt herself to be unusual. Frequently they deprecated their own views as coming from a woman's pen. And almost universally those who responded to their work felt called upon to remark upon the author's gender. The prevailing expectation was that women would not write philosophy, and it was probably no accident that so many of the women who did write and publish philosophy came from the nobility or even royalty. Class status undoubtedly made it easier for them to get their views a hearing. Perhaps it is also unusual that only one of these women, Catherine Trotter Cockburn, was the mother of a large family. The others were either childless or had only one child. In an age before birth control, most women could not expect to be so little troubled by maternal duties.

But although there were factors that in general worked against women participating in intellectual endeavors, there were others that—although not going so far as to encourage—at least went some way toward facilitating their participation. The growing tendency to publish in the vernacular was a clear benefit. But most importantly, it was not necessary during this period to possess any particular set of credentials or to belong to a specific profession in order to enter into philosophical debate. There were, as well, a number of acceptable forms in which philosophical discussion was carried out, at least some of which were relatively easy to engage in. Furthermore, the sort of gatekeepers that surround contemporary philosophical publication were unknown. Books were by and large printed and sold by booksellers, who tended to encourage rapid exchange of ideas in the form of pamphlets, controversies, and the like. In addition much philosophical dialogue took place in letters, which were often circulated or printed, providing a semi-public form of debate. It seems to have been possible, moreover, for a woman such as Mary Astell to introduce herself by letter to a philosopher—in her case, the English Malbranchian, John Norris—and to carry on an extensive correspondence, which was eventually published. The philosophical treatises of the period, which we read today, are only one kind of philosophical discussion and they took place against a background of these various other forms of philosophical activity. Reading the work of these women helps to give a flavor of the variety of ways in which ideas were exchanged.

One factor that may have made it easier for women to express themselves on philosophical issues was the way in which philosophical questions were joined to theological questions in this period. Inasmuch as the care of one's soul was everyone's concern—even a woman's—women may have felt entitled and even obliged to have an opinion on religious matters. It is perhaps no accident that, although they interested themselves in a number of issues under debate, many of these women were particularly interested in drawing the theological consequences of the matters under discussion. It may be that women felt free to participate in philosophical endeavors because such activity held the promise of adding to knowledge that would aid them in their religion. This religious motivation may well have been a liberating force in the intellectual careers of some of these women.

Another factor that may have made it easier for women to see themselves—and to be seen—as capable of doing philosophy was the view of the nature of human reason and the method of doing philosophy that stemmed from Descartes. Descartes encouraged the idea that sound reasoning was in the power of every human soul and that what was required in order to bring it about was not erudition but a method based on introspection, and hence within the means even of women. This account of reason and its implications for women is a theme that Astell and Masham explicitly take up. Astell, for example, in *A Serious Proposal to the Ladies*, Part I, argues in favor of the value of education for women, pointing out that "All have not leisure to learn languages, and pore on books, nor opportunity to converse with the learned; but all may *think*, may use their own faculties rightly, and consult the master who is within them."[1] Her claim is that education does not require the kind of book learning that men have enjoyed, but rather a proper understanding of the nature of one's rational faculties. In this, she seems to have learned a lesson Descartes was eager to teach.[2]

Whatever the motivations that may have led these women to write philosophy, it is important to emphasize that they were involved in ongoing philosophical debate, and that they did so by accepted means. Moreover, each of them was able to find a place within a recognized philosophical community. They were able to find men who treated their ideas seriously and respectfully. Many of these women were recognized, in their lifetime, for their intellectual accomplishments. If their views have been forgotten, it cannot be attributed directly to any bias against women existing at the time they wrote. More complicated factors have been at work, including the tendency among philosophers to forget all but a very few thinkers.

Although Mary Astell, in particular, and Damaris Masham and Margaret Cavendish as well may be said to have had a special concern for the position of women, they, like the other women writing philosophy, took a lively interest in the debates of the day. All of them framed their issues in the same terms as their male counterparts. Many of the seventeenth-century women interested themselves in the metaphysical issues concerning the status of material substance. We are accustomed to posing these issues in the terms laid down by Descartes, who proposed that it was the nature of body to be extended and that all corporeal states followed from this nature, while it was the nature of mind to think, thus sharply distinguishing the two. Some of the contributors to this work specifically developed their ideas in terms of the way in which Descartes put forward this distinction. Princess Elisabeth is the best example. In her letters to Descartes, she raises the question of how a thinking entity can bring about changes in a body—as it apparently does in cases of voluntary action—if the thinking soul is unextended.

The writings of some of the other women, however, remind us in a salutary manner that debates on these matters were also developed and carried out independently of Descartes. Margaret Cavendish is a good case in point. Although she reflects on Descartes in her *Philosophical Letters,* she does not owe her position to him. The view she puts forward is materialist. That is, she holds that there is a single substance but that it is corporeal in nature. She maintains, however, that this corporeal substance is capable of self-motion. Thus, she is taking a position in an important seventeenth-century debate: if matter is conceived—as Descartes believes—as extended, or even as extended and solid, then it seems to be inert in its nature. It then becomes a serious problem to explain how matter can move. Ann Conway represents a different seventeenth-century position on this issue, one that she shares with, among others, her mentor, Henry More. Because she thinks that the only natural way to explain the existence of motion is in mental or spiritual terms, she holds that there is only one substance, and that it is incorporeal in nature. Lady Masham's letters to Leibniz concern his own claims about the nature of mind and body, that each follows the laws of its own nature, but that a preestablished harmony between the two makes it appear that communication is taking place. Masham is particularly troubled by Leibniz's supposition that there can be substances that are unextended, that have no spatial location. What the ideas of these various seventeenth-century women fill in for us is the richness of the existing debates about the nature of matter, its relation to the soul, and its capacity for motion.

The interests of the remaining women are more disparate, but if there is a continuous thread running through the readings it is epistemological in nature. An important theme in seventeenth-century philosophy is the extent or limits of knowledge. Some argue—like Descartes—that our faculties are such as to give us certain knowledge, while others, like Locke, argue that the nature of our faculties is such that our capacity for knowledge is more limited. In the eighteenth century, there were various attempts to avoid the skeptical consequences of this line of reasoning, either by redefining the nature of knowledge, as Berkeley does, or by shifting the question to the scope of our faculties, as does Hume. Women entered into this debate in a variety of ways. Mary Astell, as mentioned, shares Descartes's interest in laying out rules for right reasoning, but she does not share his confidence in our native abilities. She is concerned to show that, whatever its shortcomings, we can rely on our reason, when properly used, as a guide to action. Catherine Trotter Cockburn is interested in defending a view of moral knowledge, and she carries out her project in a variety of ways. In the selection included, Trotter Cockburn shows that Locke's claim that we are not in a position to know whether or not matter can think, given our idea of matter and our idea of thought, is not a threat to belief in the immortality of the soul. Mary Shepherd, writing considerably later, also focuses on an epistemological issue, but in her case the concern centers on what she sees as the skepticism run rampant in the arguments of Berkeley and Hume. She wants to reinstate a traditional belief in the existence of an external world and in causation, which she sees as undermined by the approaches they take. Again, what we find in the writings of these women are examples of the wide variety of positions found within the epistemological debates of the period.

In making selections for this anthology, I have chosen portions of each woman's work that comment on the writings of the philosophers typically included in history of modern philosophy courses. In so doing, I do not want to imply that the writings of these women are exclusively commentaries on the work of men. This is far from the case. Rather, I have been guided by what I see as a pedagogical need: Making possible the inclusion of the study of these women without unduly disrupting an already crowded course in the history of modern philosophy. It is my hope that these brief selections will whet the appetite for a more inclusive study of these women's work, which would remedy any distorting element that may have been introduced in the editing process. In my introductory remarks to each selection, I have given a short account of each woman's life, explained something of the nature of her philosophical work, and provided some background for each selection.

Notes

1. *A Serious Proposal,* p. 98.

2. Others have seen the influence of Descartes as more pernicious, arguing that he put forward a conception of reason that excluded women. See in particular, Susan Bordo, *The Flight to Objectivity: Essays on Cartesianism and Culture* (Albany: State University of New York Press, 1987) and Genevieve Lloyd, *The Man of Reason: "Male" and "Female" in Western Philosophy* (Minneapolis: University of Minnesota Press, 1987). I have argued against this conception in "Cartesian Reason and Gendered Reason" in *A Mind of One's Own: Feminist Essays on Reason and Objectivity,* edited by Louise M. Antony and Charlotte Witt (Boulder: Westview Press, 1993).

Princess Elisabeth
of Bohemia

PRINCESS ELISABETH OF BOHEMIA was born on December 26, 1618, and died on February 8, 1680. She was the daughter of Frederick V, Elector Palatine, and Elisabeth Stuart. Her parents were for a brief time the King and Queen of Bohemia, but they were almost immediately deposed, and as a result of this adventure, lost the Palatinate and went into exile in Holland. Elisabeth was brought up by her grandmother and her aunt in Silesia, but, at the age of nine, rejoined her parents and their growing family in Holland. She was to be eventually one of thirteen children; her youngest sister Sophie grew up to be the electress of Hanover and patroness of Leibniz. Elisabeth seems to have been carefully educated. In addition to the accomplishments of music, dancing, and art, she learned Latin, seems to have been taught some natural science, and so immersed herself in the study of Ancient Greek that the family nickname for her was "La Greque." She never married, and one can imagine that it would not have been easy to have found a husband for a dowerless and militantly Protestant princess. She spent her early adulthood living in the homes of various relatives, as would have been appropriate for an unmarried woman, but around 1661, she finally achieved her own establishment. She became associated with a Protestant convent at Herford, where she served first as coadjutrix and then in 1667 as abbess. This was a position of some importance, entitling her to be styled princess of the Holy Roman Empire, and giving her both independence and occupation. She served as abbess until her death, after a long illness, in 1680.

Elisabeth's reputation as a philosopher rests on her correspondence with René Descartes, whom she met at her parents' court while she was still a young woman living in Holland. It is worth noting that in the seventeenth century, the exchange of letters was an important way in which the philosophic community exchanged and advanced ideas. Descartes kept copies of his letters to Elisabeth and occasionally would allow others to read portions of their correspondence. Elisabeth, however, does not seem to have regarded her letters as public documents, and, after Descartes's death, refused permission to have them published with the rest of his correspondence. In her letters to Descartes, we do not find Elisabeth putting forward a fully developed philosophical position, but, instead, she comments critically on the works of Descartes and others she had been reading. Indeed, as one letter makes clear, even the time to do this much is snatched from the demands made upon a woman in her position. In a letter of September 30, 1645, she wrote to Descartes: "Since I have written this, I have been interrupted more than seven times by inconvenient visitors" (Blom, p. 156).

I have included that portion of the correspondence for which Elisabeth is best known, that concerning the relationship between the mind and the body. It is generally agreed that Elisabeth pushes Descartes hard on this matter and that his responses to her contain some interesting novelties, in particular, that of the mind-body union as a "simple notion." Other matters Elisabeth raised with Descartes in letters not reprinted here included problems concerning free will and a lengthy examination of the nature of the sovereign good, on which topic Descartes advised her to read Seneca. Descartes's *Passions of the Soul* is said to derive from his conversations with Elisabeth, and he thought sufficiently well of her to dedicate his magnum opus, *The Principles of Philosophy*, to her.

✧ Selections from her
Correspondence with Descartes

extended / nonextended

ELISABETH TO DESCARTES

The Hague, 6/16 May 1643

Monsieur,

I have learned, with very great joy and regret, the intention you had to see me a few days ago, and I have been equally moved, both by your charity in consenting to communicate with an ignorant and indocile person, and by the misfortune that stole me away from so profitable a conversation. M. Pollot greatly augmented this latter passion by repeating to me the solution you gave him of the obscurities in the physics of M. Regius, concerning which I would have been better instructed from your own mouth, as also about a question I proposed to the said professor when he was in this city, and in regard to which he directed me back to you to receive the required satisfaction. The shame of showing you so unruly a style has prevented me to date from asking this favor of you by letter.

But today M. Pollot gave me such assurance of your good will toward everyone, and especially toward me, that, banishing every other consideration from mind, save that of availing myself of it, I beseech you tell me how the soul of man (since it is but a thinking substance) can determine the spirits of the body to produce voluntary actions. For it seems every determination of movement happens from an impulsion of the thing moved, according to the manner in which it is pushed by that which moves it, or else, depends on the qualification and figure of the superficies of this latter. Contact is required for the first two conditions, and extension for the third. You entirely exclude extension from your notion of the soul, and contact seems to

---

Selections from John J. Blom (trans.), *Descartes: His Moral Philosophy and Psychology* (New York: New York University, 1978), 105–116.

me incompatible with an immaterial thing. That is why I ask of you a definition of the soul more particular than in your metaphysic—that is to say, for a definition of the substance separate from its action, thought. For although we suppose them inseparable (which nonetheless is difficult to prove regarding infants in their mother's womb and deep faints), still, like the attributes of God, we can, by considering them separately, acquire a more perfect idea of them.

Knowing you to be the best doctor for my soul, I therefore freely reveal to you the weaknesses of its speculations, and I trust that in observing the oath of Hippocrates you will furnish it remedies without publicizing them; that I ask of you, as likewise, that you bear these importunities of . . . etc.

DESCARTES TO ELISABETH

Egmond du Hoef, 21 May 1643

Madame,

The favor with which Your Highness has honored me, in granting me receive her commands in writing, surpasses anything I had ever dared hope for; and it compensates for my flaws better than would that which I passionately desired—to receive those commands from your lips had I been able to be admitted to the honor of paying you reverence, and of offering you my very-humble services, when I was last at the Hague. For I would have had too many marvels to admire at the same time; and seeing a discourse more than human flow from a frame so similar to those painters bestow upon angels, I would have been ravished, just as, it seems to me, are bound to be they who, in coming from earth, enter for the first time upon heaven. In such wise was I rendered less capable of responding to Your Highness— who undoubtedly already noticed this flaw in me—when I previously had the honor of speaking to her; and it is your clemency that has wished to compensate for that flaw by placing the traces of your thoughts upon paper, where, rereading them several times, and accustoming myself to consider them, I am indeed less dazzled, yet have only so much the more admiration for them, recognizing that they do not seem ingenious merely at *what is the nature of their union?*

first sight, but proportionately more judicious and solid the further one examines them.

And I can in all honesty say that the question Your Highness proposes seems to me that which can be asked with the greatest justification in sequel to the writings I have published. For, there being two things in the human soul on which depends all the knowledge we can have of its nature—the first, that it thinks, and the second, that being united to the body, it can act and suffer with it—I have said nearly nothing of this latter, and have studied only to understand well the first, since my principal design was to prove the distinction that exists between the soul and the body, for which the first alone could suffice, while the other would have been an impediment. But since Your Highness is so discerning that one cannot hide anything from her, I shall try here to explain the manner in which I conceive the union of the soul with the body, and how it has the force to move the body.

Firstly, I consider that in us are certain primitive notions that are like originals on whose model we form all our other knowledge. And there are but very few such notions; for, after the most general ones—of being, number, duration, etc.—which refer to everything we can conceive, we have, as regards body in particular, only the notion of extension, from which follow those of figure and movement; and, as regards the soul alone, we have only that of thought, in which are comprised the perceptions of the understanding and the inclinations of the will; finally, for the soul and the body together, we have only that of their union, on which depends that of the force of the soul for moving the body, and of the body for acting upon the soul by causing its feelings and passions.

I consider also that all human knowledge consists only in carefully distinguishing these notions, and in attributing each of them only to the things to which they pertain. For when we wish to explain some difficulty by means of a notion that does not pertain to it, we cannot fail to make a mistake. And that occurs whenever we wish to explain one of these notions by another—for since they are primitive, each of them cannot be understood except through itself. And inasmuch as the use of the senses has rendered the notions of extension, figures, and movements very much more familiar to us than the others, the principal cause of our errors consists in that we ordinarily wish to employ them to explain things to which they do not pertain, as when one wishes to employ the imagination to conceive the nature of the soul, or else, when one wishes to conceive the manner in which the soul moves the body after the fashion in which a body is moved by another body.

That is why, having tried to clarify in the *Meditations* Your Highness has deigned to read, the notions that pertain to the soul alone and distinguish them from those that pertain to the body alone, the first thing I should in sequel explain is the manner of conceiving whatever pertains to the union of the soul with the body, leaving aside things that pertain to the body alone or to the soul alone. In this regard it seems to me that what I wrote at the end of my Response to the sixth objections can be of use; for we cannot seek these simple notions other than in our soul—in our soul which, although it has all of them in it by its nature, does not always sufficiently distinguish them one from another, or else fails to attribute them to the objects to which they should be attributed.

Thus I believe that we hitherto confused the notion of the force by which the soul acts on the body with that by which one body acts upon another; and that we have attributed both, not to the soul, for as yet we did not recognize it, but to different qualities of bodies, such as weight, heat, and so forth which we imagined as being real—or, as having an existence distinct from that of body, and consequently as being substances, although we called them qualities. And in order to conceive them, we have sometimes used the notions that are in us for knowing body, and sometimes those that are for knowing the soul, according as what we attributed to them has been material or immaterial. For example, in supposing weight a real quality, of which we possess no other knowledge save that it has the force of moving the body in which it exists toward the center of the earth, we have no difficulty conceiving how it moves this body, nor how it is joined to it; and we do not think that happens by means of an actual touching of one surface against another, for we experience in our own selves that we have a particular notion for conceiving it; yet I believe that in applying this notion to weight—which, as I hope to show in physics, is nothing really distinct from body—we are abusing what has been given us for conceiving the manner in which the soul moves the body.

I would show myself insufficiently aware of the incomparable wit of Your Highness if I employed more words in explaining myself, and I would be too presumptuous if I dared think my response ought satisfy her entirely; but I shall try to avoid both by adding nothing further here save that, if I am capable of writing or saying anything that can be agreeable to her, I will always consider it a very great favor to take up my pen or to go to the Hague on such account; and that there is nothing in the world so dear to me as to obey her commands. But I can find no room here for observing the oath of Hippocrates as she enjoins me; for she has communicated nothing to me that does not merit being seen and admired by all. I can only say, regarding this matter, that infinitely esteeming your letter, I shall treat it as misers do their treasures—which they stash away all the more they esteem them, and, by begrudging everyone else the sight of them, take their sovereign contentment in looking upon them. And thus I shall be very willing to enjoy all to myself the good of looking upon it; and my greatest ambition is to be able to say, and truly to be, . . . etc.

ELISABETH TO DESCARTES

The Hague, 10/20 June 1643

Monsieur Descartes,

Your good will not only shows forth, as I had been given to understand it would, in pointing out and correcting the flaws in my reasoning, but also in that, to render my recognizing them less annoying, you try—to the prejudice of your judgment—to console me by means of false praises that would have been necessary to encourage me to take the remedy had not my nourishment, in a place where the ordinary fashion of conversation has accustomed me to hear praises from persons incapable of speaking the truth, led me to suppose I could never err in believing the opposite of their discourse, and thereby to render reflection upon my imperfections so familiar as to cause me no more emotion than I require in connection with the desire to rid myself of them.

That makes me confess, without shame, that I have discovered in myself all the causes of error you note in your letter, and that I have been as yet unable to banish them entirely, since the life I am constrained to lead does not allow me enough free time to acquire a habit of meditation in accordance with your rules. Sometimes the interests of my household, which I must not neglect, sometimes conversations and civilities I cannot eschew, so thoroughly deject this weak mind with annoyances or boredom that it remains, for a long time afterward, useless for anything else: which will serve, I hope, to excuse my stupidity in being unable to comprehend, from what you had previously said concerning weight, the idea by which we should judge how the soul (nonextended and immaterial) can move the body; nor why this power, that you have then under the name of quality falsely attributed to it as carrying the body toward the center of the earth, ought persuade us that body can be pushed by something immaterial any more than the demonstration of a contrary truth (as you promise in your physics) confirms us in the opinion of its impossibility; principally, because this idea (not being able to claim to the same perfection and objective reality as that of God) can be feigned out of ignorance of what truly moves these bodies toward the center; and then, since no material cause presents itself to the senses, one would have attributed it—which I have only been able to conceive as a negation of matter—to its contrary, the immaterial, which cannot have any communication with it.

And I admit it would be easier for me to concede matter and extension to the soul, than the capacity of moving a body and of being moved, to an immaterial being. For, if the first occurred through 'information', the spirits that perform the movement would have to be intelligent, which you accord to nothing corporeal. And although in your metaphysical meditations you show the possibility of the second, it is, however, very difficult to comprehend that a soul, as you have described it, after having had the faculty and habit of reasoning well, can lose all of it on account of some vapors, and that, although it can subsist without the body and has nothing in common with it, is yet so ruled by it.

But, since you have undertaken to instruct me, I entertain these opinions only as friends that I do not intend to keep, assuring myself you will explain the nature of an immaterial substance and the manner of its actions and passions in the body just as well as all the other things you have wished to teach. I ask you also to believe there is no one upon whom you can bestow this charity more aware of the obligation she owes you for it than . . . etc.

DESCARTES TO ELISABETH

Egmond du Hoef, 28 June 1643

Madame,

I am very greatly obliged to Your Highness in that, having experienced from my preceding remarks that I badly explain myself concerning the question it has pleased her to propose to me, she again deigns to have the patience to listen to me regarding the same subject, and to give me an opportunity to note the things I had omitted. The principal omissions seem to be that, having distinguished three kinds of ideas or primitive notions, each of which are recognized in a particular manner and not by the comparison of one with another, namely, the notion we have of the soul, of the body, and of the union existing between the soul and the body, I should have explained the difference that exists among these three sorts of notions, and among the operations of the soul by which we have them, and should have stated the means of rendering each of them familiar and easy for ourselves; then, in sequel, having said why I used the comparison to weight, I should have made it plain that, although one wishes to conceive the soul as material (which is properly to conceive its union with the body), one cannot fail to recognize afterward that it is separable from it. That, I believe, is everything Your Highness has enjoined me discuss here.

First, then, I note a great difference among these three kinds

mactical wisdom

of notions, in that the soul conceives itself only by the pure understanding; body—that is to say, extension, figures, and movements—can likewise be recognized by the understanding alone, but very much better by the understanding aided by the imagination; and finally, the things that pertain to the union of the soul and the body are recognized only obscurely by the understanding alone or even by the understanding as aided by the imagination; yet they are known very clearly by the senses. From that it comes about that those who never philosophize, and who make use only of their senses, do not doubt that the soul moves the body and the body acts upon the soul; but they consider the one and the other as a single thing, that is to say, they conceive their union; for to conceive the union existing between two things is to conceive them as one thing alone. The metaphysical thoughts that exercise the pure understanding serve to render the notion of the soul more familiar to us; and the study of mathematics, which principally exercises the imagination in considering figures and movements, accustoms us to form very distinct notions of body; and finally, it is by availing oneself only of life and ordinary conversations, and by abstaining from meditating and studying things that exercise the imagination, that one learns to conceive the union of the soul and the body.

I almost fear that Your Highness may think I am not speaking seriously here; but that would be contrary to the respect I owe her and shall never fail to render her. And I can truly say that the principal rule I have always observed in my studies, and of which I believe I have made very good use in acquiring some knowledge, has been that I have never employed save very few hours each day at thoughts that occupy the imagination, and very few hours per year at those that occupy the understanding alone, and that I have devoted all the rest of my time to the respite of my senses and the repose of my mind; I even reckon among the exercises of the imagination all serious conversations, and everything that requires attention. That is what made me retire to the country. For although, were I in the most densely occupied city in the world, I could have as many more hours to myself as I now employ at studying, nevertheless I could not so usefully employ them, since my soul would be wearied by the attention required by the bustle of life. And I here take liberty of writing to Your Highness to testify to her how truly I admire that, among the affairs and cares never relenting for persons who are at once of great mind and great birth, she has yet been able to devote herself to the meditations required to recognize well the distinction that exists between the soul and the body.

But I have judged that it was those meditations, rather than thoughts that require less attention, that have made her find obscurity in the notion we have of their union; for it does not seem to me that the human mind is capable of conceiving very distinctly, and at the same time, both the distinction between the soul and the body, and also their union; because to do so it is necessary to conceive them as one thing alone, and at the same time to conceive them as two, which is the contrary. And for this reason (supposing Your Highness still had the reasons that prove the distinction of the soul and the body very present to her mind, and not wishing to ask her to rid herself of them in order to represent the notion that everyone always experiences in himself without philosophizing—namely, that it is one person alone who, at the same time, has a body and thought of such nature that this thought can move the body and feel the accidents that happen to it), I previously made use of the comparison with weight and other qualities we commonly imagine united to some body, just as thought is united to ours; and I am not concerned that this comparison limped in that such qualities are not real, as one is wont to image them, because I believed Your Highness was already entirely persuaded that the soul is a substance distinct from the body.

But, since Your Highness notes it is easier to attribute matter and extension to the soul than to attribute to it, when it has no matter, a capacity to move a body and be moved by one, I ask her to please freely attribute this matter and this extension to the soul; for that is nothing but to conceive it united to the body. And having conceived that well, and having experienced it in herself, it will be easy for her to appreciate that the matter she shall have attributed to this thought is not thought itself, but rather that the extension of this matter is of another nature than the extension of this thought, in that the first is determined to a certain place, from which it excludes every other extension of body, which the second does not. And thus Your Highness will not fail to return easily to the knowledge of the distinction of the soul and the body, notwithstanding that she has conceived their union.

Finally, just as I believe it very necessary, once in one's life, to have well understood the principles of metaphysics, since it is they that provide us with knowledge of God and our soul, I also believe it would be very harmful to occupy one's understanding in frequently meditating upon them because it could not be so healthy to abandon the functions of the imagination and senses; but the best procedure is to content oneself with retaining in one's memory and belief those conclusions one has once extracted from them, and then to devote the rest of the time remaining for studying to thoughts wherein the understanding acts along with the imagination and the senses.

My extreme devotion to the service of Your Highness makes me hope my frankness will not be disagreeable to her, and it would have led me to engage here in a longer discourse, wherein I would have tried to clarify on this occasion all the difficulties attaching to the question proposed; but troublesome news from Utrecht, where the magistrate summons me to verify what I have written about one of their ministers—that he is indeed a man who has most scandalously calumniated me, and that what I have written about him in my just defense is only too well known to everyone—compels me to finish here, in order to go consult about the means of extricating myself, as soon as possible, from these chicaneries.* I am, . . . etc.

ELISABETH TO DESCARTES

The Hague, 1 July 1643

Monsieur Descartes,

I see that my regard for your instructions, and the desire to avail myself of them, does not inconvenience you as much as does the ingratitude of they who deprive themselves, and would

---

*Descartes was summoned to defend what he had written in his *Epistle to Voetius*.

wish deprive all mankind, of them; nor would I have dispatched this new effect of my ignorance before knowing you acquitted of that of their bigotedness, except that M. Van Bergen obliged me write sooner by his civility in resolving to remain in this city until I should give him a response to your letter of 28 June in which you clearly point out the three sorts of notions we possess, their objects, and the manner of using them properly.

I too find that the senses show me that the soul moves the body; but they fail to teach me (any more than the understanding and the imagination) the manner in which she does it. And, in regard to that, I think there are unknown properties in the soul that might suffice to reverse what your metaphysical meditations, with such good reasons, persuaded me concerning her inextension. And this doubt seems founded upon the rule you lay down there in speaking of the true and the false—namely, that all our errors occur from forming judgments about what we do not sufficiently perceive. Although extension is not necessary to thought, yet not being contradictory to it, it will be able to belong to some other function of the soul less essential to her. At least that avoids the contradiction of the scholastics— namely, that the entire soul is in the entire body and entirely in each of its parts. I do not excuse myself for confusing the notion of the soul with that of the body for the same reason as do ordinary people; but that does not dispel for me the first doubt, and I will despair of finding certitude in any matter unless you provide me with it—you who alone have prevented me from being the skeptic I was inclined to be by my first reasoning.

Although I owe you this admission, by way of rendering you thanks, I should nevertheless think it very imprudent, except that I know, as much from the experience I have already had of them as by reputation, that your good will and generosity equal the rest of your merits. You cannot give witness of them in any more obliging manner than by the elucidations and advice you share with me, and which I prize above the greatest treasures that could be possessed by . . . etc.

Margaret Cavendish, Duchess of Newcastle

MARGARET CAVENDISH was born, probably in 1623, into a large, landowning family. Her father died when she was two years old, but the family fortunes were held together by the management skills of her mother. Her mother did not, however, find it necessary to provide much of an education for her daughters, and Cavendish complained of having had an inadequate education at the hands of a decayed gentlewoman. She was, however, driven from early childhood by a desire to write, filling a large number of what she later referred to as "baby books." In the quarrel between Charles I and Parliament, Cavendish's family sided with the king, and she became a lady in waiting to Queen Henrietta Maria, eventually following her into exile in France. There she met and married William Cavendish, then marquis of Newcastle, another Royalist in exile and a man considerably her senior. The marquis, like his brother, Sir Charles Cavendish, was a "virtuoso," a dabbler in the New Science. While in exile, he and his wife met and entertained Hobbes, Gassendi, Descartes, and Huygens. Cavendish fell into the habit of writing copiously, and, supported in this by her husband, publishing what she wrote. In all, she published a dozen works in a variety of forms, including poetry, plays, stories, her autobiography and the biography of her husband, and several volumes of natural philosophy. Returning to England after the Restoration, she and her husband lived mostly in the country, but, during a stay in London, Cavendish made a notorious visit to the Royal Society, the only woman to have done so. She died in 1673, predeceasing her husband, and, although she was his second wife, they lie buried together in Westminster Abbey.

In her earliest writings, Cavendish put forward a kind of atomism, holding that the ultimate constituents of the world were indivisible bits of uniform stuff, but her settled view, described in *Philosophical Letters, Observations upon Experimental Philosophy*, and *Grounds of Natural Philosophy*, was a kind of organic materialism. Nature is eternal, infinite, but above all corporeal. Being corporeal, it can be divided into parts, although these parts are not other than nature. Cavendish speaks sometimes of a hierarchy of matter, distinguishing a sensitive and rational matter, which is purer and finer, from an inanimate matter. But although she thinks it necessary to speak of an inanimate matter, to explain the slowness of some natural events, she is insistent that motion does not exist apart from matter. The belief in immaterial substance, she holds, comes from abstracting motion from matter and making it a separate entity, which entity, if immaterial, would be clearly supernatural. She suggests that the rejection of self-moving matter and the belief in immaterial substance come from human ambition: People are unwilling to see themselves as part of nature but wish to be special and Godlike. Instead, "all and every particular creature, as also all perception and variety in Nature, is made by corporeal self-motion, which I name sensitive and rational matter, which is life and knowledge, sense and reason" (*Philosophical Letters*, preface). This picture of nature as internally self-regulating is occasionally expressed in charmingly feminine language: "Nature, being a wise and provident lady, governs her parts very wisely, methodically, and orderly: Also, she is very industrious and hates to be idle, which makes her employ her time as a good housewife doth" (*Observations*, p. 102).

In the book from which this selection comes, *Philosophical Letters*, Cavendish adopts an epistolary form, which if not widely used in philosophy, was for her extremely successful. She imagines a correspondent, a woman, who is raising questions on the works of several contemporary authors, Hobbes, Descartes, Henry More, and van Helmont. Cavendish is selective in the portions of the works on which she is willing to comment, avoiding, for example, all of the political aspects of Hobbes's *Leviathan*, on the grounds that she is not qualified to speak on such a topic. She admits she was not able to read Descartes directly because she was unable to read Latin (or French) but instead "had some few places translated to me out of his works" (*Philosophical Letters*, preface). It is not clear what passages she is speaking of, as she discusses issues coming from a range of Descartes's work, including his account of motion, aspects of his theory of the relationship between mind and body, and his view that animals are not rational, a matter on which Descartes had corresponded with her husband.

✧ Selections from
Philosophical Letters

XXX

Madam,

I am reading now the works of that famous and most renowned author, Descartes, out of which I intend to pick out only those discourses which I like best, and not to examine his opinions, as they go along from the beginning to the end of his books; and in order to this, I have chosen in the first place, his discourse of motion, and do not assent to his opinion, when he defines motion to be only a mode of a thing, and not the thing or body itself; for, in my opinion, there can be no abstraction made of motion from body, neither really, nor in the manner of our

---

Selections from Margaret Cavendish, *Philosophical Letters* (London, 1664), 97–128.

conception, for how can I conceive that which is not, nor cannot be in nature, that is, to conceive motion without body? Wherefore motion is but one thing with body, without any separation or abstraction soever. Neither doth it agree with my reason, that one body can give or transfer motion into another body; and as much motion it gives or transfers into that body, as much loses it: As for example, in two hard bodies thrown against one another, where one, that is thrown with greater force, takes the other along with it, and loses as much motion as it gives it. For how can motion, being no substance, but only a mode, quit one body, and pass into another? One body may either occasion, or imitate another's motion, but it can neither give nor take away what belongs to its own or another body's substance, no more then matter can quit its nature from being matter; and therefore my opinion is, that if motion doth go out of one body into another, then substance goes too; for motion, and substance or body, as aforementioned, are all one thing, and then all bodies that receive motion from other bodies, must needs increase in their substance and quantity, and those bodies which impart or transfer motion, must decrease as much as they increase: Truly, madam, that neither motion nor figure should subsist by themselves, and yet be transferable into other bodies, is very strange, and as much as to prove them to be nothing, and yet to say they are something. The like may be said of all others, which they call accidents, as skill, learning, knowledge, etc. Saying, they are no bodies, because they have no extension, but inherent in bodies or substances as in their subjects; for although the body may subsist without them, yet they being always with the body, body and they are all one thing: And so is power and body, for body cannot quit power, nor power the body, being all one thing. But to return to motion, my opinion is, that all matter is partly animate, and partly inanimate, and all matter is moving and moved, and that there is no part of nature that hath not life and knowledge, for there is no part that has not a commixture of animate and inanimate matter; and though the inanimate matter has no motion, nor life and knowledge of itself, as the animate has, nevertheless being both so closely joined and commixed as in one body, the inanimate moves as well as the animate, although not in the same manner; for the animate moves of itself, and the inanimate moves by the help of the animate, and thus the animate is moving and the inanimate moved; not that the animate matter transfers, infuses, or communicates its own motion to the inanimate; for this is impossible, by reason it cannot part with its own nature, nor alter the nature of inanimate matter, but each retains its own nature; for the inanimate matter remains inanimate, that is, without self-motion, and the animate loses nothing of its self-motion, which otherwise it would, if it should impart or transfer its motion into the inanimate matter; but only as I said heretofore, the inanimate works or moves with the animate, because of their close union and commixture; for the animate forces or causes the inanimate matter to work with her; and thus one is moving, the other moved, and consequently there is life and knowledge in all parts of nature, by reason in all parts of nature there is a commixture of animate and inanimate matter: and this life and knowledge is sense and reason, or sensitive and rational corporeal motions, which are all one thing with animate matter without any distinction or abstraction, and can no more quit matter, then matter can quit motion. Wherefore every creature being composed of this commixture of animate and inanimate matter, has also self-motion, that is life and knowledge, not that there is any more place then body; as for example, water being mixed with earth, the water doth not take the earth's place, but as their parts intermix, so do their places, and as their parts change, so do their places, so that there is no more place, then there is water and earth; the same may be said of air and water, or air and earth, or did they all mix together; for as their bodies join, so do their places, and as they are separated from each other, so are their places. Say a man travels a hundred miles, and so a hundred thousand paces; but yet this man has not been in a hundred thousand places, for he never had any other place but his own, he hath joined and separated himself from a hundred thousand, nay millions of parts, but he has left no places behind him. You will say, if he travel the same way back again, then he is said to travel through the same places. I answer, It may be the vulgar way of expression, or the common phrase;

but to speak properly, after a philosophical way, and according to the truth in nature, he cannot be said to go back again through the same places he went, because he left none behind him, or else all his way would be nothing but place after place, all the hundred miles along; besides if place should be taken so, as to express the joining to the nearest bodies which compass him about, certainly he would never find his places again; for the air being fluid, changes or moves continually, and perchance the same parts of the air, which compassed him once, will never come near him again. But you may say, if a man be hurt, or hath some mischance in his body, so as to have a piece of flesh cut out, and new flesh growing there; then we say, because the adjoining parts do not change, that a new piece of flesh is grown in the same place where the former flesh was, and that the place of the former flesh cut or fallen out, is the same of this new grown flesh. I answer, in my opinion, it is not, for the parts being not the same, the places are not, but every one hath its own place. But if the wound be not filled or closed up with other new flesh, you will say, that according to my opinion there is no place then at all. I say, yes, for the air or any thing else may be there, as new parts joining to the other parts; nevertheless, the air, or that same body which is there, hath not taken the flesh's place, which was there before, but hath its own; but, by reason the adjoining parts remain, man thinks the place remains there also which is no consequence. 'Tis true, a man may return to the same adjoining bodies, where he was before, but then he brings his place with him again, and as his body, so his place returns also, and if a man's arm be cut off, you may say, there was an arm heretofore, but you cannot say properly, this is the place where the arm was. But to return to my first example of the mixture of water, and earth or air; suppose water is not porous, but only dividable, and hath no other place but what is its own bodies, and that other parts of water intermix with it by dividing and composing; I say, there is no more place required, then what belongs to their own parts, for if some contract, others dilate, some divide, others join, the places are the same according to the magnitude of each part or body. The same may be said of all kinds or sorts of mixtures, for one body hath but one place; and so if many parts of the same nature join into one body and increase the bulk of the body, sense and reason, so that no part hath need to give or receive motion to or from another part; although it may be an occasion of such a manner of motion to another part, and cause it to move thus or thus: as for example, a watchmaker doth not give the watch its motion, but he is only the occasion, that the watch moves after that manner, for the motion of the watch is the watch's own motion, inherent in those parts ever since that matter was, and if the watch ceases to move after such a manner or way, that manner or way of motion is nevertheless in those parts of matter, the watch is made of, and if several other figures should be made of that matter, the power of moving in the said manner or mode, would yet still remain in all those parts of matter as long as they are body, and have motion in them. Wherefore one body may occasion another body to move so or so, but not give it any motion, but everybody (though occasioned by another, to move in such a way) moves by its own natural motion; for self-motion is the very nature of animate matter, and is as much in hard, as in fluid bodies, although your author denies it, saying, the nature of fluid bodies consists in the motion of those little insensible parts into which they are divided, and the nature of hard bodies, when those little particles joined closely together, do rest; for there is no rest in nature; wherefore if there were a world of gold, and a world of air, I do verily believe, that the world of gold would be as much interiously active, as the world of air exteriously; for nature's motions are not all external or perceptible by our senses, neither are they all circular, or only of one sort, but there is an infinite change and variety of motions; for though I say in my philosophical opinions, as there is but one only matter, so there is but one only motion; yet I do not mean, there is but one particular sort of motions, as either circular, or straight, or the like, but that the nature of motion is one and the same, simple and entire in itself, that is, it is mere motion, or nothing else but corporeal motion; and that as there are infinite divisions or parts of matter, so there are infinite changes and varieties of motions, which is the reason that I call motion as well infinite as matter; first that matter and motion are but one thing, and if matter be infinite, motion must be so too; and secondly, that motion is infinite in its changes and variations, as matter is in its parts. And thus much of motion for this time; I add no more, but rest,

MADAM,

Your faithful friend,
and servant.

XXXI

Madam,

I observe your author in his discourse of place makes a difference betwixt an interior and exterior place, and that according to this distinction, one body may be said to change, and not to change its place at the same time, and that one body may succeed into another's place. But I am not of this opinion, for I believe the place of that same body is accordingly; and if they be bodies of different natures which intermix and join, each several keeps its place; and so each body and each particular part of a body hath its place, for you cannot name body or part of a body, but you must also understand place to be with them, and if a point should dilate to a world, or a world contract to a point, the place would always be the same with the body. And thus I have declared my opinion of this subject, which I submit to the correction of your better judgment, and rest,

MADAM,

Your ladyship's
faithful friend and humble servant.

XXXII

Madam,

In my last, I hope, I have sufficiently declared my opinion, that to one body belongs but one place, and that no body can leave a place behind it, but wheresoever is body, there is place also. Now give me leave to examine this question: when a body's figure is printed on snow, or any other fluid or soft matter, as air, water, and the like; whether it be the body, that prints its own figure upon the snow, or whether it be the snow, that patterns the figure of the body? My answer is, that it is not the body, which prints its figure upon the snow, but the snow that patterns out the figure of the body; for if a seal be printed upon wax, 'tis true, it is the figure of the seal, which is printed on the wax, but yet the seal doth not give the wax the print of its own figure, but it is the wax that takes the print or pattern from the seal, and patterns or copies it out in its own substance, just as the sensitive motions in the eye do pattern out the figure of an object, as I have declared heretofore. But you will say, perhaps, a body being printed upon snow, as it leaves its print, so it leaves also its place with the print in the snow. I answer, that doth not follow; for the place remains still the body's place, and when the body removes out of the snow, it takes its place along with it: Just like a man, whose picture is drawn by a painter, when he goes away, he leaves not his place with his picture, but his place goes with his body; and as the place of the picture is the place of the color or paint, and the place of the copy of an exterior object patterned out by the sensitive corporeal motions is the place of the sensitive organ, so the place of the print in snow, is the snow's place; or else, if the print were the body's place that is printed, and not the snow's, it might as well be said, that the motion and shape of a watch were not the motion and shape of the watch, but of the hand of him that made it. And as it is with snow, so it is with air, for a man's figure is patterned out by the parts and motions of the air, wheresoever he moveth; the difference is only, that air being a fluid body doth not retain the print so long, as snow or a harder body doth, but when the body removes, the print is presently dissolved. But I wonder much, your author denies, that there can be two bodies in one place, and yet makes two places for one body, when all is but the motions of one body: Wherefore a man failing in a ship, cannot be said to keep place, and to change his place; for it is not place he changes, but only the adjoining parts, as leaving some, and joining to others; and it is very improper, to attribute that to place which belongs to parts, and to make a change of place out of change of parts. I conclude, repeating once again, that figure and place are still remaining the same with body; for example; let a stone be beat to dust, and this dust be severally dispersed, nay, changed into numerous figures; I say, as long as the substance of the stone remains in the power of those dispersed and changed parts, and their corporeal motions, the place of it continues also; and as the corporeal motions change and vary, so doth place, magnitude and figure, together with their parts or bodies, for they are but one thing. And so I conclude, and rest,

MADAM,

Your faithful friend,
and servant.

XXXIII

Madam,

I am absolutely of your author's opinion, when he says, that all bodies of this universe are of one and the same matter, really divided into many parts, and that these parts are diversly moved: But that these motions should be circular more then of any other sort, I cannot believe, although he thinks that this is the most probable way, to find out the causes of natural effects: for nature is not bound to one sort of motions more then to another, and it is but in vain to endeavour to know how, and by what motions God did make the world, since creation is an action of God, and God's actions are incomprehensible; wherefore his ethereal whirlpools, and little particles of matter, which he reduceth to three sorts and calls them the three elements of the universe, their circular motions, several figures, shavings, and many the like, which you may better read, then I rehearse to you, are to my thinking, rather fancies, then rational or probable conceptions: for how can we imagine that the universe was set a moving as a top by a whip, or a wheel by the hand of a spinster, and that the vacuities were filled up with shavings? For these violent motions would rather have disturbed and disordered nature; and though nature uses variety in her motions or actions, yet these are not extravagant, nor by force or violence, but orderly, temperate, free, and easy, which causes me to believe, the earth turns about rather then the sun; and though corporeal motions for variety make whirlwinds, yet whirlwinds are not constant, neither can I believe that the swiftness of motion could make the matter more subtle and pure then it was by nature, for it is the purity and subtlety of the matter, that causes motion, and makes it swifter or slower, and not motion the subtlety and purity of matter; motion being only the action of matter; and the self-moving part of matter is the working part of nature, which is wise, and knows how to move and form every creature without instruction; and this self-motion is as much her own as the other parts of her body, matter and figure, and is one and the same with herself, as a corporeal, living, knowing, and inseparable being, and a part of herself. As for the several parts of matter, I do believe, that they are not all of one and the same bigness, nor of one and the same figure, neither do I hold their figures to be unalterable; for if all parts in nature be corporeal, they are dividable, composable, and intermixable, and then they cannot be always of one and the same sort of figure; besides nature would not have so much work if there were no change of figures: and since her only action is change of motion, change of motion must needs make change of figures: and thus natural parts of matter may change from lines to points, and from points to lines, from squares to circles, and so forth, infinite ways, according to the change of motions; but though they change their figures, yet they cannot change their matter; for matter as it has been, so it remains constantly in each degree, as the rational, sensitive and inanimate, none becomes purer, none grosser then ever it was, notwithstanding the infinite changes of motions, which their figures undergo; for motion changes only the figure, not the matter itself, which continues still the same in its nature, and cannot be altered without a confusion or destruction of nature. And this is the constant opinion of,

MADAM,
Your faithful friend,
and humble servant.

XXXIV

Madam,

That rarefaction is only a change of figure, according to your author's opinion, is in my reason very probable; but when he says, that in rarified bodies are little intervals or pores filled up with some other subtle matter, if he means that all rarified bodies are porous, I dissent from him; for it is not necessary that all rarified bodies should be porous, and all hard bodies without pores: but if there were a probability of pores, I am of opinion, it would be more in dense and hard, than in rare and soft bodies; as for example, rarifying and dilating motions are planing, smoothing, spreading and making all parts even, which could not well be, if there were holes or pores; earth is dense and hard, and yet is porous, and flame is rare and dilating, and yet is not porous; and certainly water is not so porous as earth. Wherefore pores, in my opinion, are according to the nature or form of the figure, and not according to the rarity or thinness, and density or thickness of the substance. As for his thin and subtle matter filling up the pores of porous bodies, I assent to your author so far that I mean, thin and thick, or rare and dense substances are joined and mixed together. As for planing, smoothing and spreading, I do not mean so much artificial planing and spreading; as for example, when a piece of gold is beaten into a thin plate, and a board is made plane and smooth by a joiner's tool, or a napkin folded up is spread plane and even, although, when you observe these arts, you may judge somewhat of the nature of natural dilations; for a folded cloth is fuller of creases then when plane, and the beating of a thin plate is like to the motion of dilation, which is to spread out, and the form of rarifying is thinning and extending. I add only this, that I am not of your author's opinion, that rest is the cause or glue which keeps the parts of dense or hard bodies together, but it is retentive motions. And so I conclude, resting,

MADAM,
Your faithful friend,
and servant.

XXXV

Madam,

That the mind, according to your author's opinion, is a substance really distinct from the body, and may be actually separated from it and subsist without it: If he mean the natural mind and soul of man, not the supernatural or divine, I am far from his opinion; for though the mind moveth only in its own parts, and not upon, or with the parts of inanimate matter, yet it cannot be separated from these parts of matter, and subsist by its self, as being a part of one and the same matter the inanimate is of, (for there is but one only matter, and one kind of matter, although of several degrees,) only it is the self-moving part; but yet this cannot empower it, to quit the same natural body, whose part it is. Neither can I apprehend, that the mind's or soul's seat should be in the *glandula* or kernel of the brain, and there sit like a spider in a cobweb, to whom the least motion of the cobweb gives intelligence of a fly, which he is ready to assault, and that the brain should get intelligence by the animal spirits as his servants, which run to and fro like ants to inform it; or that the mind should, according to others' opinions, be a light, and embroidered all with ideas, like a herald's coat; and that the sensitive organs should have no knowledge in themselves, but serve only like peeping-holes for the mind, or barn doors to receive bundles of pressures like sheaves of corn; for there being a thorough mixture of animate, rational and sensitive, and inanimate matter, we cannot assign a certain seat or place to the rational, another to the sensitive, and another to the inanimate, but they are diffused and intermixed throughout all the body; and this is the reason, that sense and knowledge cannot be bound only to the head or brain: But although they are mixed together, nevertheless they do not lose their interior natures by this mixture, nor their purity and subtlety, nor their proper motions or actions, but each moves according to its nature and substance, without confusion; the actions of the rational part in man, which is the mind or soul, are called thoughts, or thoughtful perceptions, which are numerous, and so are the sensitive perceptions; for though man, or any other animal hath but five exterior sensitive organs, yet there be numerous perceptions made in these sensitive organs, and in all the body; nay, every several pore of the flesh is a sensitive organ, as well as the eye, or the ear. But both sorts, as well the rational as

the sensitive, are different from each other, although both do resemble another, as being both parts of animate matter, as I have
mentioned before: Wherefore I'll add no more, only let you
know, that I constantly remain,

MADAM,

Your faithful friend,
and servant.

XXXVI

Madam,

That all other animals, besides man, want reason, your author endeavours to prove in his discourse of method, where his
chief argument is, that other animals cannot express their mind,
thoughts or conceptions, either by speech or any other signs, as
man can do: For, says he, it is not for want of the organs belonging to the framing of words, as we may observe in parrots and
'pies, which are apt enough to express words they are taught, but
understand nothing of them. My answer is, that one man ex-
pressing his mind by speech or words to another, doth not de-
clare by it his excellency and supremacy above all other creatures, but for the most part more folly, for a talking man is not so
wise as a contemplating man. But by reason other creatures cannot speak or discourse with each other as men, or make certain
signs, whereby to express themselves as dumb and deaf men do,
should we conclude, they have neither knowledge, sense, reason,
or intelligence. Certainly, this is a very weak argument; for one
part of a man's body, as one hand, is not less sensible then the
other, nor the heel less sensible than the heart, nor the leg less
sensible then the head, but each part hath its sense and reason,
and so consequently its sensitive and rational knowledge; and
although they cannot talk or give intelligence to each other by
speech, nevertheless each hath its own peculiar and particular
knowledge, just as each particular man has his own particular
knowledge, for one man's knowledge is not another man's
knowledge; and if there be such a peculiar and particular knowledge in every several part of one animal creature, as man, well

may there be such in creatures of different kinds and sorts: But this particular knowledge belonging to each creature, doth not prove that there is no intelligence at all betwixt them, no more then the want of human knowledge doth prove the want of reason; for reason is the rational part of matter, and makes perception, observation, and intelligence different in every creature, and every sort of creatures, according to their proper natures, but perception, observation and intelligence do not make reason, reason being the cause, and they the effects. Wherefore though other creatures have not the speech, nor mathematical rules and demonstrations, with other arts and sciences, as men; yet may their perceptions and observations be as wise as men's, and they may have as much intelligence and commerce betwixt each other, after their own manner and way, as men have after theirs: To which I leave them, and man to his conceited prerogative and excellence, resting,

MADAM,
Your faithful friend,
and servant.

XXXVII

Madam,

Concerning sense and perception, your author's opinion is, that it is made by a motion or impression from the object upon the sensitive organ, which impression, by means of the nerves, is brought to the brain, and so to the mind or soul, which only perceives in the brain; explaining it by the example of a man being blind, or walking in dark, who by the help of his stick can perceive when he touches a stone, a tree, water, sand, and the like; which example he brings to make a comparison with the perception of light; for, says he, light in a shining body, is nothing else but a quick and lively motion or action, which through the air and other transparent bodies tends toward the eye, in the same manner as the motion or resistance of the bodies, the blind man meets withal, tends through the stick toward the hand; wherefore it is no wonder that the sun can display its rays so far in an instant, seeing that the same action, whereby one end of the stick is moved, goes instantly also to the other end, and would do the same if the stick were as long as heaven is distant from earth. To which I answer first, that it is not only the mind that perceives in the kernel of the brain, but that there is a double perception, rational and sensitive, and that the mind perceives by the rational, but the body and the sensitive organs by the sensitive perception; and as there is a double perception, so there is also a double knowledge, rational and sensitive, one belonging to the mind, the other to the body; for I believe that the eye, ear, nose, tongue, and all the body, have knowledge as well as the mind, only the rational matter, being subtle and pure, is not encumbered with the grosser part of matter, to work upon, or with it, but leaves that to the sensitive, and works or moves only in its own substance, which makes a difference between thoughts, and exterior senses. Next I say, that it is not the motion or reaction of the bodies, the blind man meets withal, which makes the sensitive perception of these objects, but the sensitive corporeal motions in the hand do pattern out the figure of the stick, stone, tree, sand, and the like. And as for comparing the perception of the hand, when by the help of the stick it perceives the objects, with the perception of light, I confess that the sensitive perceptions do all resemble each other, because all sensitive parts of matter are of one degree, as being sensible parts, only there is a difference according to the figures of the objects presented to the senses; and there is no better proof for perception being made by the sensitive motions in the body, or sensitive organs, but that all these sensitive perceptions are alike, and resemble one another; for if they were not made in the body of the sentient, but by the impression of exterior objects, there would be so much difference betwixt them, by reason of the diversity of objects, as they would have no resemblance at all. But for a further proof of my own opinion, did the perception proceed merely from the motion, impression and resistance of the objects, the hand could not perceive those objects, unless they touched the hand itself, as the stick doth; for it is not probable, that the motions of the stone, water, sand, etc. should leave their bodies and enter into the stick, and so into the hand; for motion must be either something or nothing; if something, the stick and the hand would grow bigger, and the objects touched less, or else the touching and the touched must exchange their motions, which cannot be done so suddenly, especially between solid bodies; but if motion has no body, it is nothing, and how nothing can pass or enter or move some body, I cannot conceive. 'Tis true there is no part that can subsist singly by itself, without dependence upon each other, and so parts do always join and touch each other, which I am not against; but only I say perception is not made by the exterior motions of exterior parts of objects, but by the interior motions of the parts of the body sentient. But I have discoursed hereof before, and so I take my leave, resting,

MADAM,
Your faithful friend,
and servant.

XXXVIII

Madam,

I cannot conceive why your author is so much for little and insensible parts, out of which the elements and all other bodies are made; for though nature is dividable, yet she is also composable; and I think there is no need to dissect every creature into such little parts, to know their nature, but we can do it by another way as well; for we may dissect or divide them into never so little parts, and yet gain never the more knowledge by it. But according to these principles he describing amongst the rest the nature of water, says, that those little parts, out of which water consists, are in figure somewhat long, light and slippery like little eels, which are never so closely joined and entangled, but may easily be separated. To which I answer, that I observe the nature and figure of water to be flowing, dilating, dividable and circular; for we may see, in tides, overflowings, and breaking into parts, as in rain, it will always move in a round and circular figure; and I think, if its parts were long and entangled like a knot of eels, it could never be so easily contracted and densed into snow or ice. Neither do I think, that saltwater hath a mixture of somewhat grosser parts, not so apt to bend; for to my observation and reason, the nature of saltwater consists herein, that its circle lines are pointed, which sharp and pointed figure makes it so penetrating; yet may those points be separated from the circle lines of water, as it is seen in the making of salt. But I am not of your author's opinion, that those little points do stick so fast in flesh, as little nails, to keep it from putrefaction; for points do not always fasten; or else fire, which certainly is composed of sharp-pointed parts, would harden, and keep other bodies from dissolving, whereas on the contrary, it separates and divides them, although after several manners. But putrefaction is only a dissolving and separating of parts, after the manner of dilation; and the motion of salt is contracting as well as penetrating, for we may observe, what flesh soever is dry-salted doth shrink and contract close together; I will not say, but the pointed parts of salt may fasten like nails in some sorts of bodies, but not in all they work on. And this is the reason also, that seawater is of more weight then fresh-water, for being composed of points, those points stick within each other, and so become more strong; but yet do they not hinder the circular dilating motion of water, for the circle lines are within, and the points without, but only they make it more strong from being divided by other exterior bodies that swim upon it. And this is the cause that saltwater is not so easily forced or turned to vapor, as fresh, for the points piercing into each other, hold it more strongly together; but this is to be considered, that the points of salt are on the outside of the watery circle, not on the inside, which causes it to be dividable from the watery circles. I will conclude, when I have given the reason why water is so soon sucked up by sand, lime, and the like bodies, and say that it is the nature of all spongy, dry and porous bodies, meeting with liquid and pliable bodies as water, do draw and suck them up, like as animal creatures being thirsty, do drink: and so I take my leave, and rest,

  MADAM,
    Your faithful friend,
      and servant.

XXXIX

Madam,

Concerning vapor, clouds, wind and rain, I am of your author's opinion, that water is changed into vapor, and vapor into air, and that dilated vapors make wind, and condensed vapors, clouds and mists; but I am not for his little particles, whereof, he says, vapors are made, by the motion of a rare and subtle matter in the pores of terrestrial bodies; which certainly I should conceive to be loose atoms, did he not make them of several figures and magnitude: for, in my opinion, there are no such things in nature, which like little flies or bees do fly up into the air; and although I grant, that in nature are several parts, whereof some are more rare, others more dense, according to the several degrees of matter, yet they are not single, but all mixed together in one body, and the change of motions in those joined parts, is the cause of all changes of figures whatever, without the assistance of any foreign parts: and thus water of itself is changed to snow, ice, or hail, by its inherent figurative motions; that is, the circular dilation of water by contraction, changes into the figure of snow, ice, or hail; or by rarifying motions it turns into the figure of vapor, and this vapor again by contracting motions into the figure of hoarfrost; and when all these motions change again into the former, then the figure of ice, snow, hail, vapor and frost, turns again into the figure of water: and this in all sense and reason is the most facile and probable way of making ice, snow, hail, etc. As for rarefaction and condensation, I will not say that they may be forced by foreign parts, but yet they are made by change and alteration of the inherent motions of their own parts, for though the motions of foreign parts, may be the occasion of them, yet they are not the immediate cause or actors thereof. And as for thunder, that clouds of ice and snow, the uppermost being condensed by heat, and so made heavy, should fall upon another and produce the noise of thunder, is very improbable; for the breaking of a little small string, will make a greater noise than a huge shower of snow with falling, and as for ice being hard, it may make a great noise, one part falling upon another, but then their weight would be as much as their noise, so that the clouds or roves of ice would be as soon upon our heads, if not sooner, as the noise in our ears; like as a bullet shot out of a cannon, we may feel the bullet as soon as we hear the noise. But to conclude, all condensations are not made by heat, nor all noises by pressures, for sound is oftener made by division then pressure, and condensation by cold then by heat: And this is all for the present, from,

MADAM,

Your faithful friend,
and servant.

XL

Madam,

I cannot perceive the rational truth of your author's opinion, concerning colors, made by the agitation of little spherical bodies of an ethereal matter, transmitting the action of light; for if colors were made after this manner, there would, in my opinion, not be any fixed or lasting color, but one color would be so various, and change faster then every minute; the truth is, there would be no certain or perfect color at all: wherefore it seems altogether improbable, that such liquid, rare and disunited bodies should either keep or make inherent and fixed colors; for liquid and rare bodies, whose several parts are united into one considerable bulk of body, their colors are more apt to change then the colors of those bodies that are dry, solid and dense; the reason is, that rare and liquid bodies are more loose, slack, and agile, then solid and dry bodies, in so much, as in every alteration of motion their colors are apt to change: and if united rare and liquid bodies be so apt to alter and change, how is it probable, that those bodies, which are small and not united; should either keep or make inherent fixed colors? I will not say, but that such little bodies may range into such lines and figures, as make colors, but then they cannot last, being not united into a lasting body, that is, into a solid, substantial body, proper to make such figures as colors. But I desire you not to mistake me, madam, for I do not mean, that the substance of colors is a gross thick substance, for the substance may be as thin and rare as flame or light, or in the next degree to it; for certainly the substance of light, and the substance of colors come in their degrees very near each other; but according to the contraction of the figures, colors are paler or deeper, or more or less lasting. And as for the reason, why colors will change and rechange, it is according as the figures alter or recover their forms; for colors will be as animal creatures, which sometimes are faint, pale, and sick, and yet recover; but when as a particular color is, as I may say, quite dead, then there is no recovering of it. But colors may seem altered sometimes in our eyes, and yet not be altered in themselves; for our eyes, if perfect, see things as they are presented; and for proof, if any animal should be presented in an unusual posture or shape, we could not judge of it; also if a picture, which must be viewed side-wards, should be looked upon forwards, we could not know what to make of it; so the figures of colors, if they be not placed rightly to the sight, but turned topsy-turvy as the phrase is, or upside down, or be moved too quick, and this quick motion do make a confusion with the lines of light, we cannot possibly see the color perfectly. Also several lights or shades may make colors appear otherwise then in themselves they are, for some sorts of lights and shades may fall upon the substantial figures of colors in solid bodies, in such lines and figures, as they may overpower the natural or artificial inherent colors in solid bodies, and for a time make other colors, and many times the lines of light or of shadows will meet and sympathize so with inherent colors, and place their lines so exactly, as they will make those inherent colors more splendorous then in their own nature they are, so that light and shadows will add or diminish or alter colors very much. Likewise some sorts of colors will be altered to our sight, not by all, but only by some sorts of light, as for example, blue will seem green, and green blue by candlelight, when as other colors will never appear changed, but show constantly as they are; the reason is, because the lines of candlelight fall in such figures upon the inherent colors, and so make them appear according to their own figures; wherefore it is only the alteration of the exterior figures of light and shadows, that make colors appear otherwise, and not a change of their own natures; and hence we may rationally conclude, that several lights and shadows by their spreading and dilating lines may alter the face or outside of colors, but not suddenly change them, unless the power of heat, and continuance of time, or any other cause, do help and assist them in that work of metamorphosing or transforming of colors; but if the lines of light be only, as the phrase is, skin-deep; that is, but lightly spreading and not deeply penetrating, they may soon wear out or be rubbed off; for though they hurt, yet they do not kill the natural color, but the color may recover and reassume its former vigor and lustre: but time and other accidental causes will not only alter, but destroy particular colors as well as other creatures, although not all after the same manner, for some will last longer than others. And thus, madam, there are three sorts of colors, natural, artificial, and accidental; but I have discoursed of this subject more at large in my philosophical opinions, to which I refer you, and rest,

MADAM,
Your faithful friend,
and servant.

XLI

Madam,

My answer to your author's question, why flame ascends in a pointed figure is, that the figure of fire consists in points, and being dilated into a flame, it ascends in lines of points slopeways from the fired fuel; like as if you should make two or more sticks stand upright and put the upper ends close together, but let the lower ends be asunder, in which posture they will support each other, which, if both their ends were close together, they could not do. The second question is, why fire doth not always flame? I answer, because all fuel is not flamable, some being so moist, as it doth oppose the fire's dryness, and some so hard and retentive, as fire cannot so soon dissolve it; and in this contest, where one dissipates, and the other retains, a third figure is produced, viz. smoke, between the heat of one, and the moisture of the other; and this smoke is forced by the fire out of the fuel, and is nothing else but certain parts of fuel, raised to such a degree of rarefaction; and if fire come near, it forces the smoke into flame, the smoke changing itself by its figurative motions into flame; but when smoke is above the flame, the flame cannot force the smoke to fire or enkindle itself, for the flame cannot so well encounter it; which shows, as if smoke had a swifter motion than flame, although flame is more rarified then smoke; and if moisture predominate, there is only smoke, if fire, then there is flame: But there are many figures, that do not flame, until they are quite dissolved, as leather, and many other things. Neither can fire work upon all bodies alike, but according to their several natures, like as men cannot encounter so several sorts of creatures after one and the same manner; for not any part in nature hath an absolute power, although it hath self-motion; and this is the reason, that wax by fire is melted, and clay hardened. The third question is, why some few drops of water sprinkled upon fire, do encrease its flame? I answer, by reason of their little quantity, which being overpowered by the greater quantity and force of fire, is by its self-motions converted into fire; for water being of a rare nature, and fire, for the most part, of a rarifying quality, it cannot suddenly convert itself into a more solid body then its nature is, but following its nature by force it turns into flame. The fourth question is, why the flame of spirit of wine doth consume the wine, and yet cannot burn or hurt a linen cloth? I answer, the wine is the fuel that feeds the flame, and upon what it feeds, it devoureth, and with the food, the feeder; but by reason wine is a rarer body then oil, or wood, or any other fuel, its flame is also weaker. And thus much of these questions, I rest,

MADAM,

Your faithful friend,
and servant.

XLII

Madam,

To conclude my discourse upon the opinions of these two famous and learned authors, which I have hitherto sent you in several letters, I could not choose but repeat the ground of my own opinions in this present; which I desire you to observe well, least you mistake anything, whereof I have formerly discoursed. First I am for self-moving matter, which I call the sensitive and rational matter, and the perceptive and architectonical part of nature, which is the life and knowledge of nature. Next I am of an opinion, that all perception is made by corporeal, figuring self-motions, and that the perception of foreign objects is made by patterning them out: as for example, the sensitive perception of foreign objects is by making or taking copies from these objects, so as the sensitive corporeal motions in the eyes copy out the objects of sight, and the sensitive corporeal motions in the ears copy out the objects of sound; the sensitive corporeal motions in the nostrils, copy out the objects of scent; the sensitive corporeal motions in the tongue and mouth, copy out the objects of taste, and the sensitive corporeal motions in the flesh and skin of the body copy out the foreign objects of touch; for when you stand by the fire, it is not that the fire, or the heat of the fire enters your flesh, but that the sensitive motions copy out the objects of fire and heat. As for my book of philosophy, I must tell you, that it treats more of the production and architecture of creatures than of their perceptions, and more of the causes than the effects, more in a general then peculiar way, which I thought necessary to inform you of, and so I remain,

MADAM,

Your faithful friend,
and servant.

Anne Viscountess Conway

ANNE VISCOUNTESS CONWAY was born December 14, 1631, and died in 1678 at the age of 47. She was born into a prominent family and although educated at home, she does not seem to have been discouraged from intellectual pursuits, but, among other things, learned Latin and Greek. She was in fact encouraged in this by her brother, John Finch, who introduced her to his tutor at Cambridge, Henry More, the Cambridge Platonist, with whom Conway formed a close friendship. In 1651, she married Edward Conway, Viscount Conway, who had also been a pupil of More's. Throughout her life, Conway suffered from a very debilitating form of headache, probably a version of migraine, and in consequence lived a very quiet life in the country at Ragley Hall, where she was frequently visited by More and others of his circle. It was in the pursuit of a cure for her headaches that Conway met the second important influence in her life, Francis Mercury van Helmont, the son of the "proto-chemist," Jean Baptiste van Helmont, who was persuaded to come to Ragley to try and cure Conway's headaches. Although he was able to work only a slight and temporary alleviation of her pain, he remained at Ragley for nine years, until Conway's death. Initially More and van Helmont shared along with Conway in some intellectual interests, in particular in the Cabalistic writings of Christian Knorr von Rosenroth. In time, however, van Helmont became increasingly interested in Quakerism, and eventually persuaded Conway to formally join the Quakers. Not long after her conversion, she died after days of terrible pain. Her brother wrote of her: "I must never hope to see again in this world, knowledge enough to have made a man of parts proud, in a more talkative sex to be possessed without noise."

Anne Conway's treatise, *The Principles of the Most Ancient and Modern Philosophy,* has a rather checkered history. After her death, van Helmont carried away from Ragley a philosophical notebook that Conway had written, but had never revised. It is said to have been prepared for publication and translated into Latin under the joint editorship of van Helmont and More, and was eventually published in 1690 in Holland along with some other material belonging to van Helmont. This Latin treatise was subsequently retranslated into English, and published in England in 1692. Anne Conway's original English version being lost, this retranslation was published by Peter Loptson in 1982, although it is now out of print. Because, upon leaving Anne Conway, van Helmont visited Leibniz to whom he conveyed his good opinion of Conway's thought and to whom he might have shown her work, there has been speculation that Leibniz was influenced by Conway. Leibniz himself contributed to this notion, writing to Thomas Burnett that "My philosophical views approach somewhat closely those of the late Countess of Conway." It is likely, however, that any coincidence in their views stems from ideas "in the air" rather than any transference from Conway to Leibniz, as Leibniz's opinions on the relevant topics had been formed before he could have read Anne Conway's treatise, if indeed, he ever did.

Anne Conway's theory is, as far as nature goes, both monist and vitalist. She distinguishes three distinct kinds of being, God, Christ, and creation, which are differentiable from each other chiefly with respect to changeability—God is utterly unchangeable, Christ is changeable only for the better, and hence forms a necessary mediation between God and creation, and creatures are changeable for better or for worse. With respect to creatures, this feature has the result that any creature could in principle be transformed into any other. Conway emphasizes that what is distinctive about her claim is not that one piece of matter could be transformed into another, as the body of a horse into the body of a person, for this she recognizes as true on any seventeenth-century account of matter, but what she regards as her interesting claim is that the spirit of a horse could in principle be transformed into the spirit of a person. This is because creation is infinitely perfectible, so that, if a horse could only become as good a horse as possible and never achieve the excellence of a person, this would be a limitation of its ability to change for the better. A horse may not be as good a spiritual being as a person, as intelligent, say, but this is not because it is a different kind of spiritual being with a different kind of intelligence. In fact, Conway wants to go so far as to claim that there is no difference in kind between body and spirit, that even though in each creature there is a passive principle and an active one, the difference is only in degree not in kind. Although Conway gives a number of arguments for this thesis, the most interesting involve her rejection, as unintelligible, of Descartes's claim that there is inert matter subject only to local motion. Conway holds that there are not, as Descartes would have it, two forms of explanation for motion, one for body and one for spirits, but only one. Therefore, for Conway, the only intelligible form of explanation is vitalistic, in terms proper to spirits. Thus she distinguishes her theory from Descartes, in rejecting his dualism, and from Hobbes, in rejecting his materialism.

✧ Selections from
The Principles of the Most Ancient and Modern Philosophy

CHAP. VI

That all creatures in their own nature are changeable, the distinction between God and creatures, duly considered, evi-

---

Selections from Anne Conway, *The Principles of the Most Ancient and Modern Philosophy*, London, 1692.

dently evinces, and the same is by daily experience confirmed. Now if any creature be in its own nature changeable, it hath this mutability, as it is a creature, and consequently all creatures will have the same, according to that rule: Whatsoever agrees to any thing as placed under this or that species, agrees to all comprehended under the same species, but mutability agrees to a creature (which is the most general name of that species, under which all creatures are comprehended), and from thence it is manifest; for otherwise there would be no distinction between God and creatures: For if any creature were of itself, and in its own nature unchangeable, that creature would be God, because immutability is one of his incommunicable attributes.

Now let us consider how far this mutability may reach, or be extended; and, first, whether one individual can be changed into another of the same or a different species: This, I say, is impossible; for then the very essences of things would be changed, which would make a great confusion, not only in the creatures, but in the wisdom of God, which made all things: As for example: if this man could be changed into that, viz. Paul into Judas, or Judas into Paul, then he that sinned would not be punished for his sin, but another in his stead, who was both virtuous and innocent; so then a good man would not receive the reward of his virtue, but a vicious man in his stead: But if we suppose one good man to be changed into another, as Paul into Peter, and Peter into Paul, Paul would not receive his own proper reward, but Peter's nor Peter his, but Paul's, which would be a confusion, and unbecoming the wisdom of God. Moreover, if the very individual essences of things could be changed one into another, it would follow, creatures were not true in themselves; and so we could not be assured, nor have any certain knowledge of any thing; and then all the inbred notions and dictates of truth, which men generally find in themselves, would be false, and by consequence the conclusions drawn from thence; for every true science, or certainty of knowledge, depends upon the truth of the objects, which are commonly called *veritates objectivae*, or objective truths: If therefore these objective truths should be changed the one into the other, certainly the truth of the propositions depending thereon would be changed also; and so no proposition could be unchangeably true, no not the most clear and obvious as these are; the whole is greater than its part, and two halves make a whole.

The second thing to be considered, is whether one species of things can be changed into another? Where we must diligently observe after what manner the species of things are distinguished one from another; for there be many species of things, which are commonly so called, and yet in substance or essence differ not one from another, but in certain manners or properties, and when those modes or properties are changed, that thing is said to have changed its species: Now whether or no this be not a certain manner of existence, and not the essence or being of the thing itself that is so changed? As when water indeed is not changed, but remains the same, and cold coagulates it, which before was fluid: When water is changed into a stone, certainly there is no reason, why we should here suppose a greater change of its substance, than in the former example of water turned into ice. And again when a stone is changed into soft and tender earth, here is made no change of its substance; and so in all other mutations which we observe in things, the substance or essence always remains the same, and there is only a change of modus or manner; so that when a thing ceases to be after this manner, it then begins to be after another manner. And indeed the same reasons do prove, that one species essentially or substantially distinct from another, cannot be changed into another, even as one individual cannot be changed into another: For the species of things are nothing else but individuals digested, or comprehended, under one general idea of the mind, or common term of speaking: As a man, inasmuch as he is a species, comprehends under him all the individuals of men; and a horse is a species comprehending every individual horse. How if one man cannot be changed into another, much less can this man be changed into another individual of a differing species. For example: If Alexander cannot be changed into Darius, he cannot be changed into his own horse Bucephalus.

In order to know how far the mutation of things can reach, we must examine how many species of things there be, which as to substance or essence are distinct one from another; and if we diligently inquire thereinto, we shall find only three, as before was said, viz. God, Christ, and the creatures, and that these three in respect of essence, are really distinct one from another, is already proved, but there can be no reason alledged to prove, that there is any fourth kind of being distinct from the other three; yea, a fourth kind of being seems wholly superfluous: And because all the phenomena in the whole universe may be sufficiently resolved into these three beforementioned, as into their proper and original causes, there is no necessity to acknowledge any other, according to this rule: (Which if rightly understood, it is most true and certain) beings are not to be multiplied without necessity; for seeing the three beforementioned remove all the specifical differences in substances, which possibly can be conceived in our minds; and so by these alone is that vast and infinite possibility of things filled up: How then can there be room or place found for a fourth, fifth, sixth, or seventh being? And that it is performed by these three is already before demonstrated; to wit, that whatsoever can be in any wise called a being, the same is either wholly unchangeable, and such is God the supreme being, or is wholly changeable, viz. to good, or evil, and such is the creature or lowest being, or that which is partly unchangeable, viz. in respect of evil, or partly changeable, to wit, in respect of good; by which is understood Christ, the son of God; that middle being between God and the creatures; into what *classis* or rank therefore shall we bring a certain fourth, fifth, sixth, or seventh being, etc., which is neither wholly changeable, nor wholly unchangeable; nor partly changeable, nor partly unchangeable: Besides, he that supposeth a certain fourth being, essentially or substantially distinct from the three beforementioned, overthrows that most excellent order we find in the universality of things, to wit, that there is not only one medium between God and the creatures, but two, three, four, five, six, or as many as can be supposed between first and latter. Moreover, it is very consentaneous to sound reason, and so also to the order of things, that as God is but one, neither hath he two, three, or more distinct substances in him; and Christ but one Christ, neither hath in him more distinct substances, inasmuch as he is the heavenly man, and very first Adam; so likewise the creature, or whole creation, is but one only substance or essence in specie, although it comprehends many individuals placed in their subordinate species, and indeed in manner, but not in substance or essence distinct one from another. And so that which Paul speaketh concerning man, may in like manner be understood of all creatures, (who in their original state were a certain species of man so called for their excellencies, as hereafter shall be shown;) to wit, that God made all nations, or armies of creatures, out of one blood: And certainly here the reason of both is the same; for as God made all nations out of one blood, to the end they might love each other, and stand in a mutual sympathy, and help each other; so hath he implanted a certain universal sympathy and mutual love in creatures, as being all members of one body, and (as I may so say) brethren, having one common father, to wit, God in Christ, or the word made flesh; and so also one mother, viz. that substance or essence alone, out of which they proceeded, and whereof they are real parts and members; and albeit sin hath in a wonderful manner impaired this love and sympathy, yet it hath not destroyed it.

Those three distinct beings, beforementioned, being granted, and no more, which are wholly inconvertible the one into the other, we shall tread in a secure path, in the mid-way of truth, leaving these grand errors and confusions about entity, both on the right hand and the left: For, first, there are some, who teach, that there is but one being of all things, whereof the creatures are real and proper parts, and these confound God and the creatures together, as though both were but one single essence; so that sin and devils would be nothing else but parts, or at least modifications of that divine being, from whence do arise very dangerous consequences. Although I would not have it misinterpreted to those who are unwarily fallen into this opinion; yet I would warn the reader, that he may the better consider whereunto such principles tend, and avoid their absurdity. There are others again who allow only two species of things, viz. God the Supreme Being, wholly unchangeable; and the creature the lowest being, wholly changeable; but these do not duly consider that excellent order by us above described, which is apparent in all things; because else peradventure they would have taken notice, that besides these two extremes, there is a certain medium, which is partaker of both, and this is Jesus that Christ, whom not only the wiser sort of the Jews, but also some among the Gentiles so called, have acknowledged, viz. maintaining that there is such a medium, which they called by diverse names, as logos, the Son of God, the first begotten of God, mind, wisdom, heavenly Adam etc. So that some also do call him the eternal medium: Which things, if duly considered, may not a little conduce to the propagation and furthering of the true faith, and Christian religion, among the Jews, as well as Turks, and other infidel nations; that is to say, if it appears we are able to prove that there is a mediator between God and man; yea, between God and all creatures, by as solid reasons as those are, which prove God to be a creator: And so they that believe on that, may be said truly to believe on Christ Jesus, though they should not as yet have known, or been convicted, that he came in the flesh: For if they yield to the former, they will undoubtedly be forced (if ingenious) whether they will or no, to grant the latter. Others there are, who do as it were infinitely multiply the specifical beings of things, in their distinct essences and essential attributes; which wholly subverts that excellent order of things, and greatly obscures and darkens the glory of the divine attributes, so that it cannot shine forth in its due splendor and brightness in the creatures: For so every creature is so exceeding straitly bounded, and strictly included and imprisoned within the narrow limits of its own species, that the mutability of creatures is wholly taken away: Neither can any creature variously exercise any greater participation of divine goodness, or be advanced or promoted to any farther perfection.

All which we shall demonstrate by one or two examples: And first, let us take an horse, which is a creature endued with diverse degrees of perfection by his creator, as not only strength of body, but (as I may so say) a certain kind of knowledge, how he ought to serve his master, and moreover also love, fear, courage, memory, and diverse other qualities which are in man: which also we may observe in a dog, and many other animals: Seeing therefore the divine power, goodness, and wisdom, hath created every creature good; and indeed so, that it might by con-

tinual augmentations (in its mutability) be advanced to a greater
degree of goodness, ad infinitum, whereby the glory of those
attributes do more and more shine forth: And seeing such is the
nature of every creature, that it is always in motion or operation,
which doth most certainly tend unto an higher degree of goodness, as the reward and fruit of its labor; unless the creatures
hinder that good by a voluntary transgression, and abuse of that
indifferency of will which God placed in them in their creation.
Now I demand, unto what higher perfection and degree of
goodness, the being or essence of an horse doth or may attain after he hath done good service for his master, and so performed
his duty, and what is proper for such a creature? Is a horse then a
mere fabric or dead matter? or hath he a spirit in him, having
knowledge, sense, and love, and diverse other faculties and properties of a spirit? if he hath, which cannot be denied, what becomes of this spirit when the horse dies? if it be said it passeth
into life, and takes upon it another body of an horse, so that it
becomes a horse as before, which horse may be stronger and
fairer, and of a more excellent spirit than before. Very well! But
if he shall die, two, three, or four times, etc. shall he always remain a horse, though he be still better, and more excellent, by
how much the oftener his spirit revolves. Now I demand,
whether the spirit of an horse hath in it such infinite perfection,
that a horse may always become better and better ad infinitum,
and yet so as to remain a horse? For as the common received
opinion is, this visible earth shall not always remain in the same
state, which may be confirmed by undeniable reasons: Now it
necessarily follows, that the continual generation of animals in
these gross bodies shall cease also; for if the earth shall take on it
another form, neither any longer bring forth grass, horses and
other animals shall cease to be such as they were before: And
seeing they want their proper aliment, they cannot remain in
the same species; yet nevertheless they are not annihilated, as
may be easily conceived; for how can any thing be annihilated,
seeing the goodness of God towards his creatures always remains the same; and the conservation or continuation of creatures is a continued creation, as is generally granted, and already
before demonstrated, that God is a perpetual creator; and as he

is the most free, so also the most necessary agent: But if it be denied, that the earth is unchangeable, as before was said, then it will come to pass that horses and other animals, according to their proportion, will be in like manner changed with the earth, and the earth according to the same proportion, will again produce or yield them aliment or food agreeable to their changed condition; then I demand, Whether they shall always remain in the same species under such a change? Or, whether there will not be some difference between that state and this? As for example: There is between a cow and a horse, which is commonly granted to be specifical. Again, I ask whether the species of creatures do so infinitely one excel another, that an individual of one particular species may still go forward in perfection, and approach nearer unto another species, but yet never reach so far as to be changed into that species? As for instance: An horse in diverse qualities and perfections draws near unto the nature and species of a man, and that more than many other creatures; is therefore the nature of a man distant from the nature of an horse, by infinite degrees, or by finite only? If by finite, then certainly a horse may in length of time be in some measure changed into a man, (I mean his spirit; as for his body that is a thing evident): If infinitely distant; then unto any man, even one of the vilest and basest nature and disposition, may be attributed a certain infinite excellence in act, such as only agrees to God and Christ, but to no creature; for the highest excellence of a creature is to be infinite only, in *potentia,* not in *actu;* that is, to be still in a possibility of attaining a greater perfection and excellence, ad infinitum, though it can never reach this infinite; for how far soever an finite being may proceed, yet that is still finite, although there be no limits to its progression: As for example: if we could ever come to the least minute of eternity, or the like part of infinite duration, that would not be infinite, but finite: Neither do we herein contradict what is delivered in the third chapter, of the infiniteness of creatures; for it is not meant of their infinite goodness and excellence, but in respect only of multitude and magnitude; so that the one cannot be numbered, nor the other measured, by the comprehension of any created intellect: yet the individuals of creatures, are always but finitely good, and finitely distant, *quoad* species, or as to species; and only potentially infinite; that is, always capable of farther perfection without end. As if there should be supposed a certain ladder, which should be infinitely long, containing infinite steps, yet those steps are not infinitely distant one from another, otherwise there could be no ascension nor descension made thereon; for steps (in this example) signify the various species of things, which cannot be infinitely distant one from another, or from those which are next unto them; yea daily experience teaches us, that the species of diverse things are changed, one into another, as earth into water, and water into air, and air into fire or ether; and the contrary, as fire into air, and air into water, etc. which yet are distinct species of things; and so also stones are changed into metals, and one metal into another; but least some should say these are only naked bodies and have no spirit, we shall observe the same not only in vegetables, but also in animals, like as barley and wheat are convertible the one into the other, and are in very deed often so changed, which is well enough known to housekeepers in many provinces, and especially in Hungary, where if barley be sown wheat springs up instead thereof; but in other places more barren, and especially in rocky places, such as are found in Germany, if wheat be sown, barley cometh up, and barley in other places becomes mere grass: And in animals, worms are changed into flies, and beasts, and fishes that feed on beasts, and fishes of a different kind, do change them into their own nature, and species. And doth not also a corrupted nature, or the body of earth and water, produce animals without any previous seed of those animals? And in the creation of this world, did not the waters at the command of God, produce birds and fishes? And did not the earth also at the same command bring forth beasts and creeping things; which for that cause were real and proper parts of the earth and waters? And as they had their bodies from the earth, so likewise they had their spirits or souls from the same; for the earth brought forth living souls, as the Hebrew Text speaketh, but not mere corporeal figures, wanting life and soul; wherefore there is a very remarkable difference between human creatures and brutes: Of man it is said, God made him after his own image, and breathed into him the breath of life, and he became a living soul; so that from hence man received his life, that principal part of him, (by which he is become a man), which is really distinct from that divine soul or spirit which God breathed into him.

And seeing the body of man was made out of the earth, which (as is proved) had therein diverse spirits, and gave spirits to all brute beasts; then unto man, no doubt, She committed the best and most excellent spirits whom he was to contain; but all these spirits were of a far inferior species, in regard of the spirit of man, which he received from above, and not from the earth: And the spirit of man ought to have dominion over these spirits, (which were all but earthly), so as to subdue them to himself, and exalt them to an higher degree, (viz.) into his own proper nature, and that would have been his true increase and multiplication; for all this he suffered the earthly spirits existing within him, to get dominion over him, and so became like them; wherefore it is said, earth thou art, and unto earth thou shalt return, which hath no less a spiritual than a literal signification.

Now we see how gloriously the justice of God appears in this transmutation of things out of one species into another; and that there is a certain justice which operates not only in men and angels, but in all creatures, is most certain; and he that doth not observe the same may be said to be utterly blind: For this justice appears as well in the ascension of creatures, as in their descension; that is, when they are changed into the better, and when into the worse; when into the better, this justice distributes to them the reward and fruit of their good deeds; when into the worse, the same punishes them with due punishments, according to the nature and degree of the transgression. And the same justice hath given a law to all creatures, and written the same on their natures; and every creature whatsoever, that transgresseth this law, is punished for it: But that creature that observes and keeps it, hath this reward viz. to become better. So under the law which God gave to the Jews, if a beast killed a man, that beast was to be slain; and the life of man is said to be required at the hand of every beast, *Gen.* 9.5. And if any one had to do with a beast, not only the man, but the beast, was to be slain; so not only the woman and her husband did receive sentence and punishment from God after their transgression, but the serpent also, which was the brutish part in man, which he took from the earth. God hath also put the same instinct of justice in man, towards beasts and trees of the field; for whosoever he be that is a good and just man, the same loves his beasts that serve him, and taketh care of them that they have their food and rest, and what else is wanting to them; and this he doth not do only for his own profit, but out of a principle of true justice; for should he be so cruel to them as to require their labor, and yet deny them their necessary food, then certainly he transgresseth that law which God hath written on his heart; and if he kills any of them, only to fulfill his own pleasure, he acts unjustly, and the same measure will again be measured unto him; so likewise a man that hath a certain fruitful tree in his orchard, that prospereth well, he dungs and cleanses the same, that it may wax better and better; but if it be barren, and encumbers the ground, then he heweth it down with an ax, and burns it with fire. And so here is a certain justice in all these, as in all the transmutation of things from one species into another, whether it be by ascending from the ignobler or baser unto the nobler, or by descending into the contrary, there may be found the same justice: For example: is it not just and equitable, if a man on earth liveth a pure and holy life, like unto the heavenly angels, that he should be exalted to an angelical dignity after death, and be like unto them, over whom also the angels rejoice? But if a man here on earth lives so wickedly and perversely, that he is more like a devil raised from hell than any other creature, if he dies in such a state without repentance, shall not the same justice tumble him down to hell? and shall not such deservedly become like devils, even as those who led an angelical life are made equal with the angels? But if a man hath neither lived an angelical or diabolical, but a brutish, or at least-wise an animal or sensual life on earth; so that his spirit is more like the spirit of a beast than any other thing: Shall not the same justice most justly cause, that as he is become a brute, as to his spirit; whilst he hath left the dominion of his more excellent part, to that brutish part and spirit within him, that he also (at least, as to his external form, in bodily figure) should be changed into that species of beasts, to whom he was inwardly most like, in qualities and conditions of mind? And seeing this brutal spirit is now become superior and predominant in him, and holds the other captive, is it not very probable, when such a man dies, that the very same brutish spirit shall still have dominion in him, and carry the human soul with it whithersoever it pleaseth, and compel it to be subservient unto it? And when the said brutish spirit returns again into some body, and hath now dominion over that body, so that its plastic faculty hath the liberty of forming a body, after its own idea and inclination, (which before, in the human body, it had not); it necessarily follows, that the body, which this vital spirit forms, will be brutal, and not human; for the brutal spirit cannot produce and form any other figure: Because its plastic faculty is governed of its imagination, which it doth most strongly imagine to its self, or conceive its own proper image; which therefore the external body is necessarily forced to assume. . . .

Now therefore let us examine, how every creature is composed, and how the parts of its composition may be converted the one into the other; for that they have originally one and the same essence, or being.

In every visible creature there is a body and a spirit, or *principium magis activum,* and *magis passivum,* or, more active and more passive principle, which may fitly be termed male and female, by reason of that analogy a husband hath with his wife. For as the ordinary generation of men requires a conjunction and cooperation of male and female; so also all generations and productions whatsoever they be, require an union, and conformable operation of those two principles, to wit, spirit and body; but the spirit is an eye or light beholding its own proper image, and the body is a tenebrosity or darkness receiving that image, when the spirit looks thereinto, as when one sees himself in a lookingglass; for certainly he cannot so behold himself in the transparent air, nor in any diaphanous body, because the reflexion of an image requires a certain opacity or darkness, which we call a body: Yet to be a body is not an essential property of anything; as neither is it a property of anything to be dark; for nothing is so dark that it cannot be made light; yea, the darkness itself may become light, as the light which is created may be turned into darkness, as the words of Christ do fully evince, when he saith, if the light which is in thee be darkness, etc. where he means the eye or spirit which is in the body, which beholdeth the image of anything: Therefore as every spirit hath need of a body, that it may receive and reflect its image, so also it requires a body to retain the same; for every body hath this retentive nature, either more or less in itself; and by how much the perfecter a body is, that is, more perfectly mixed, so much the more retentive is it, and so water is more retentive than air, and earth of some things is more retentive than water.

But the seed of a female creature, by reason of its so perfect mixture; for that it is the purest extraction of the whole body, hath in it a noble retention: And in this seed, as a body, the male seed, which is the image and spirit of the male, is received and retained, together with other spirits which are in the female; and therefore whatsoever spirit is then strongest, and hath the strongest image or idea in the seed, whether it be the masculine or the feminine, or any other spirit from either of these received from without, that spirit is predominant in the seed, and forms the body, as near as may be, after its own image, and so every creature receives his external form. And after the same manner also, the internal productions of the mind, viz. thoughts are generated, which according to their kind are true creatures, and have a true substance, proper to themselves, being all our internal children, and all of them male and female, that is, they have body and spirit; for if they had not a body, they could not be retained, nor could we reflect on our own proper thoughts; for every reflection is made by a certain tenebrosity or darkness, and this is a body; so the memory requires a body, to retain the spirit of the thing thought on, otherwise it would vanish as the image in a glass, which presently vanishes, the object being removed. And so likewise, when we remember any body, we see his image in us, which is a spirit that proceeded from him, whilst we beheld him from without; which image or spirit is retained in some body, which is the seed of our brain, and thence is made a certain spiritual generation in us: And so every spirit hath its body, and every body its spirit; and as the body, *sc.* of a man or beast, is nothing else but an innumerable multitude of bodies, compacted together into one, and disposed into a certain order; so likewise the spirit of a man, or beast, is a certain innumerable multitude of spirits united together in the said body, which have their order and government so, that there is one captain, or chief governor, another a lieutenant, and another hath a certain kind of government under him, and so through the whole, as it is wont to be in an army of soldiers; wherefore the creatures are called armies, and God the God of Hosts, as the devil which possessed the man was called legion, because there were many of them; so that every man; yea, every creature, consists of many spirits and bodies; (many of these spirits which exist in man) are called by the Hebrews, Nizzuzoth, or Sparks. See in *Kabbal. denud.* Tom. 2. Part 2. Tract. *de revolutionibus animarum,* Cap. 2. and *seq.* p. 256, 268, etc.) And indeed every body is a spirit, and nothing else, neither differs any thing from a spirit, but in that it is more dark; therefore by how much the thicker and grosser it is become, so much the more remote is it from the degree of a spirit, so that this distinction is only modal and gradual, not essential or substantial.

CHAP. VIII

To prove that spirit and body differ not essentially, but gradually, I shall deduce my fourth argument from the intimate band or union, which intercedes between bodies and spirits, by means whereof the spirits have dominion over the bodies with which they are united, that they move them from one place to another, and use them as instruments in their various operations. For if spirit and body are so contrary one to another, so that a spirit is only life, or a living and sensible substance, but a body a certain mass merely dead; a spirit penetrable and indiscerpible, but a body impenetrable and discerpible, which are all contrary attributes: What (I pray you) is that which doth so join or unite them together? Or, what are those links or chains, whereby they have so firm a connection, and that for so long a space of time? Moreover also, when the spirit or soul is separated from the body, so that it hath no longer dominion or power over it to move it as it had before, What is the cause of this separation? If it be said, that the vital agreement, the soul hath to the body, is the cause of the said union, and that the body being corrupted that vital agreement ceaseth. I answer, we must first inquire, in what this vital agreement doth consist; for if they cannot tell us wherein it doth consist, they only trifle with empty words, which give a sound but want a signification: For certainly in that sense which they take body and spirit in, there is no agreement at all between them; for a body is always a dead thing, void of life and sense, no less when the spirit is in it, than when it is gone out of it: Hence there is no agreement at all between them; and if there is any agreement, that certainly will remain the same, both when the body is sound, and when it is corrupted. If they deny this, because a spirit requires an organized body, by means whereof it performs its vital acts of the external senses; moves and transports the body from place to place; which organical action ceases when the body is corrupted. Certainly by this the difficulty is never the better solved. For why doth the spirit require such an organized body? *ex. gr.* Why doth it require a corporeal eye so wonderfully formed and organized, that I can see by it? Why doth it need a corporeal light, to see corporeal objects? Or, why is it requisite, that the image of the object should be sent to it, through the eye, that it may see it? If the same were entirely nothing but a spirit, and no way corporeal, Why doth it need so many several corporeal organs, so far different from the nature of it? Furthermore, how can a spirit move its body, or any of its members, if a spirit (as they affirm) is of such a nature, that no part of its body can in the least resist it, even as one body is wont to resist another, when 'tis moved by it, by reason of its impenetrability? For if a spirit could so easily penetrate all bodies, Wherefore doth it not leave the body behind it, when it is moved from place to place, seeing it can so easily pass out without the least resistance? For certainly this is the cause of all motions which we see in the world, where one thing moves another, viz. because both are impenetrable in the sense aforesaid: For were it not for this impenetrability one creature could not move another, because this would not oppose that; nor at all resist it; an example whereof we have in the sails of a ship, by which the wind drives the ship, and that so much the more vehemently, by how much the fewer holes, vents and passages, the same finds in the sails against which it drives: When on the contrary, if instead of sails nets were expanded, through which the wind would have a freer passage; certainly by these the ship would be but little moved, although it blew with great violence: Hence we see how this impenetrability causes resistance, and this makes motion. But if there were no impenetrability, as in the case of body and spirit, then there could be no resistance, and by consequence the spirit could make no motion in the body.

And if it be objected, that God is altogether incorporeal and intrinsically present in all bodies, and yet doth move bodies whethersoever he pleaseth, and is the first mover of all things, and yet nothing is impenetrable to him: I answer, this motion by which God moves a body, doth wonderfully differ from that manner by which the soul moves the body; for the will of God which gave being to bodies, gave them motion also, so that motion itself is of God, by whose will all motion happens: for as a creature cannot give being to itself, so neither can it move itself; for in him we live, move, and have our being; so that motion and essence come from the same cause, sc. God the creator, who remains immoveable in himself; neither is he carried from place to place, because he is equally present everywhere, and gives being to creatures: But the case is far different, when the soul moves the body; for the soul is not the author of motion, but only determines it to this or that particular thing: And the soul itself is moved, together with the body, from place to place; and if the body be imprisoned, or held in chains, it cannot free or deliver itself out of prison or out of chains: Wherefore it would be a very unfit comparison, if one should go about to illustrate that motion the soul makes in the body, by an example of God moving his creatures; yea, so great is the difference, as if a man should go to demonstrate how a carpenter builds a ship, or a house, by an example of God creating the first matter or substance, wherein certainly there is as great a disparity or disproportion; for God gave being to creatures, but a carpenter doth not give being to the wood whereof he builds a ship.

But no man can think, because I have said, all motion of

creatures is of God, that therefore he is, or can be the author, or cause of sin: For although the moving power be of God, yet sin is not in the least of God, but of the creature, who hath abused this power, and determined to some other end that it ought: So that sin is ἀταξία, or an inordinate determination of motion, *or the power of moving from its due place, state, or condition unto some other, as, v.g.* a ship is moved by the wind, but governed by the mariner, that it goes to this or that place; where the mariner is not the author or cause of the wind; but the wind blowing, he makes either a good or a bad use of the same, whereby he either brings the ship to the place intended, and so is commended; or else so manages here that she suffers shipwreck, for which he is blamed, and worthy of punishment.

Moreover, why is the spirit or soul so passible in corporal pains? for if when it is united with the body, it hath nothing of corporeity, or a bodily nature, why is it grieved or wounded when the body is wounded, which is quite of a different nature? For seeing the soul can so easily penetrate the body, How can any corporeal thing hurt it? If it be said, the body only feels the pain, but not the soul; this is contrary to their own principles, because they affirm, that the body hath neither life nor sense: But if it be granted, that the soul is of one nature and substance with the body, although it is many degrees more excellent in regard of life and spirituality, as also in swiftness of motion, and penetrability, and diverse other perfections; then all the aforesaid difficulties will vanish, and it will be easily conceived, how the body and soul are united together, and how the soul moves the body, and suffers by it or with it. What the opinion of the Hebrews is appears from a place in *Kabbal. denud.* Tom. I. Part 3. Dissert. 8. Cap. 13. p. 171. *seq.*

For we may easily understand how one body is united with another, by that true agreement that one hath with another in its own nature; and so the most subtle and spiritual body may be united with a body that is very gross and thick, *sc.* by means of certain bodies, partaking of subtlety and grossness, according to divers degrees, consisting between two extremes, and these middle bodies are indeed the links and chains, by which the soul, which is so subtle and spiritual, is conjoined with a body so gross; which middle spirits (if they cease, or are absent) the union is broken or dissolved; so from the same foundation we may easily understand, how the soul moves the body, viz. as one subtle body can move another gross and thick body: And seeing body itself is a sensible life, or an intellectual substance, it is no less clearly conspicuous, how one body can wound, or grieve, or gratify, or please another; because things of one, or alike nature, can easily affect each other: And to this argument may be reduced the like difficulties, viz. how spirits move spirits; and how some spirits strive and contend with other spirits; also concerning the unity, concord, and friendship, which good spirits reverence among themselves; for if all spirits could be intrinsically present one with another, how could they dispute or contend about place? And how can one expel or drive out another? and yet that there is such an expulsion and conflict of spirits, and especially of the good against the evil, some few who have been acquainted with their own hearts have experimentally known. If it be said, the spirit of God and Christ are intrinsically present in all things, contends with, and makes war against the devil, and his spirit, in the heart of man. I answer, that this is also a very unfit similitude, (viz.) when God and creatures are compared in their operations: For his ways are infinitely superior to ours; yet nevertheless in this case also here remains a strong objection. For the spirits of God and Christ, when they strive against the devil, and the evil spirits in the heart of man, do unite themselves with certain good spirits, whom they have sanctified and prepared for this union; and by these, as a vehicle, or triumphant chariot, they contend against and encounter those malignant and wicked spirits: And in as much as these evil spirits contend against those good spirits in the heart of the man, they contend against God and Christ; and these good spirits are the spirits of this faithful and pious Man, who is become good, when as before he was evil: For God and Christ do help every pious man to prevail over the evil spirits in this conflict, but suffers the wicked and unfaithful to be captivated and overcome; for God helps none but those that fear, love, and obey him, and trust in his power, goodness, and truth; for with such he is united, and the good spirits of such men are as so many swords and darts, whereby those dark and unclean spirits are wounded and repulsed. But if it be demanded how the soul of man can be united with God, though it were in a state of the highest purity; because he is a mere spirit; but the soul even in its greatest purity always partakes of corporeity? I answer, it is done by Jesus Christ, who is the true and proper medium between both; for Christ and the soul may be united without a medium, by reason of that great affinity and similitude between them, which those doctors cannot demonstrate between spirit and body, who say they are of a nature so contrary one to another.

CHAP. IX

From what hath been lately said, and from diverse reasons alleged, that spirit and body are originally in their first substance but one and the same thing, it evidently appears that the philosophers (so called) which have taught otherwise, whether ancient or modern, have generally erred and laid an ill foundation in the very beginning, whence the whole house and superstructure is so feeble, and indeed so unprofitable, that the whole edifice and building must in time decay, from which absurd foundation have arose very many gross and dangerous errors, not only in philosophy, but also in divinity (so called) to the great damage of mankind, hindrance of true piety, and contempt of God's most glorious name, as will easily appear, as well from what hath been already said, as from what shall be said in this chapter.

And none can object, that all this philosophy is no other than that of Descartes, or Hobbes under a new mask. For first, as touching the Cartesian philosophy, this saith that every body is a mere dead mass, not only void of all kind of life and sense, but utterly uncapable thereof to all eternity; this grand error also is to be imputed to all those who affirm body and spirit to be contrary things, and inconvertible one into another, so as to deny a body all life and sense; which is quite contrary to the grounds of this our philosophy. Wherefore it is so far from being a Cartesian principle, under a new mask, that it may be truly said it is anti-Cartesian, in regard of their fundamental principles; although it cannot be denied that Descartes taught many excellent and ingenious things concerning the mechanical part of natural operations, and how all natural motions proceed according to rules and laws mechanical, even as indeed nature herself, i.e. the creature, hath an excellent mechanical skill and wisdom in itself, (given it from God, who is the fountain of all wisdom,) by which it operates: But yet in nature, and her operations, they are far more than merely mechanical; and the same is not a mere organical body, like a clock, wherein there is not a vital principle of motion; but a living body, having life and sense, which body is far more sublime than a mere mechanism, or mechanical motion.

But, secondly, as to what pertains to Hobbes's opinion, this is yet more contrary to this our philosophy, than that of Descartes; for Descartes acknowledged God to be plainly immaterial, and an incorporeal spirit. Hobbes affirms God himself to be material and corporeal; yea, nothing else but matter and body, and so confounds God and the creatures in their essences, and denies that there is any essential distinction between them. These and many more the worst of consequences are the dictates of Hobbes's philosophy; to which may be added that of Spinoza; for this Spinoza also confounds God and the creatures together, and makes but one being of both; all which are diametrically opposite to the philosophy here delivered by us.

But the false and feeble principles of some who have undertaken to refute the philosophy of Hobbes and Spinoza, so called, have given them a greater advantage against themselves; so that they have not only in effect, not refuted them, but more exposed themselves to contempt and laughter.

But if it be objected, that this our philosophy seems, at least, very like that of Hobbes, because he taught that all creatures were originally one substance, from the lowest and most ignoble, to the highest and noblest; from the smallest worm, insect, or fly, unto the most glorious angel; yea, from the least dust or sand, unto the most excellent of all creatures; and then this, that every creature is material and corporeal; yea, matter and body itself; and by consequence the most noble actions thereof, are either material and corporeal, or after a certain corporeal manner. Now I answer to the first, I grant that all creatures are originally one substance, from the lowest to the highest, and consequently convertible or changeable, from one of their natures into another; and although Hobbes saith the same, yet that is no prejudice to the truth of it, as neither are other parts of that philosophy where Hobbes affirms something that is true, therefore an Hobbism, or an opinion of Hobbes alone.

Moreover, this principle is so far from defending them in their errors, that nothing is so strong to refute them, *ex. gr.* The Hobbists argue, all things are one, because we see that all visible things may be changed one into another; yea, that all visible things may be changed into invisible, as when water is made air, and wood being burnt (for the greatest part) is changed into a certain invisible substance, which is so subtle, that it escapes all observation of our senses; add to which, that all invisible things may become visible, as when water proceeds from air, etc. and hence he concludes, nothing is so low that it cannot attain to sublimity.

But now that we may answer to this argument, his adversaries generally deny the antecedent, and on the contrary affirm that no species of things is convertible into another: And when wood is burnt, many say that the wood is composed of two substances; to wit, matter and form, and that the matter remains the same, but the form of the wood is destroyed or annihilated, and a new form of fire is produced in this matter; so that according to them, here is a continual annihilation of real substances and productions of new ones in this world: But this is so frivolous, that many others deny that, in the case of wood, changed into fire, and afterwards into smoke and ashes; yet they still persist in the same error in other transmutations, as when wood is changed into an animal, as we often see that of rotten wood; yea, dung also, living creatures are generated: But if they deny here, that the wood is changed into an animal, and say that wood is nothing but matter; but matter hath not life, nor a capacity to life or sense; and therefore this animal which hath life and sense, ought to have the same from elsewhere, and must have a spirit or soul in it, that is not a part of its body, neither doth proceed from it, but is sent thither.

But if it be demanded of them, from whence this spirit is sent, and who sendeth it; Also why a spirit of this species is sent, and not of another; here they are at a stand, and yield themselves to their adversaries.

Therefore this our philosophy before laid down, more strongly conduces to the refutation of the Hobbesian and Spinozan philosophy, viz. that all kinds of creatures may be changed into another, that the lowest may become the highest, and the highest (as considered originally in its own proper nature) may become the lowest, *sc.* according to that course and succession which divine wisdom hath ordained, that one change may succeed another in a certain order; so that A must be first turned into B, before it can be turned into C, which must be turned into C, before it can be changed into D, etc.

But we deny the consequence, viz. that God and creatures are one substance.

For in all transmutations of creatures from one species into another, as from a stone into earth, and from earth into grass, and from grass to a sheep and from a sheep into human flesh, and from human flesh into the most servile spirits of man, and from these into his noblest spirits; but there can never be a progression or ascension made unto God, who is the chiefest of all beings, and whose nature still infinitely excels a creature placed in his highest perfection; for the nature of God is every way unchangeable, so that it doth not admit of the least shadow of a change: But the nature of a creature is to be changeable.

Secondly, if it be said, by way of objection, that according to this philosophy, every creature is material and corporeal; yea, body and matter itself, as Hobbes teacheth. Now I answer, that by material and corporeal, as also by matter and body, here the thing is far otherwise understood, than Hobbes understood it, and which was never discovered to Hobbes or Descartes, otherwise than in a dream: For what do they understand by matter and body? Or, what attributes do they ascribe to them? None, certainly, but these following as are extension and impenetrability, which nevertheless are but one attribute; to which also may be referred figurability and mobility. But, suppose, these are distinct attributes, certainly this profits nothing, nor will ever help us to understand what that excellent substance is, which they call body and matter; for they have never proceeded beyond the husk or shell, nor ever reached the kernel, they only touch the superficies never discerning the center, they were plainly ignorant of the noblest and most excellent attributes of that substance which they call body and matter, and understood nothing of them. But if it be demanded, what are those more excellent attributes; I answer, these following, spirit, or life, and light, under which I comprehend a capacity of all kind of feeling, sense, and knowledge, love, joy, and fruition, and all kind of power and virtue, which the noblest creatures have or can have; so that even the vilest and most contemptible creature; yea, dust and sand, may be capable of all those perfections, *sc.* through various and succedaneous transmutations from the one into the other; which according to the natural order of things, require long periods of time for their consummation, although the absolute power of God (if it had pleased him) could have accelerated or hastened all things, and effected it in one moment: But this wisdom of God saw it to be more expedient, that all things should proceed in their natural order and course; so that after this manner, that fertility or fruitfulness, which he hath endued every being with, may appear, and the creatures have time by working still to promote themselves to a greater perfection, as the instruments of divine wisdom, goodness and power, which operates in, and with them; for therein the creature hath the greater joy, when it possesseth what it hath, as the fruit of its own labor.

But this capacity of the aforementioned perfections is quite a distinct attribute from life, and understanding, or knowledge, quite distinct from the former, viz. extension and figure; and so also a vital action is plainly distinct from local, or mechanical motion, although it is not nor cannot be separated from it, but still useth the same at least, as its instrument, in all its concourse with the creatures.

I say, life and figure are distinct attributes of one substance, and as one and the same body may be transmuted into all kinds of figures; and as the perfecter figure comprehends that which is more imperfect; so one and the same body may be transmuted from one degree of life to another more perfect, which always comprehends in it the inferior. We have an example of figure in a triangular prism, which is the first figure of all right lined solid bodies, whereinto a body is convertible; and from this into a cube, which is a perfecter figure, and comprehends in it a prism; from a cube it may be turned into a more perfect figure, which comes nearer to a globe, and from this into another, which is yet nearer; and so it ascends from one figure, more imperfect, to another more perfect, ad infinitum; for here are no bounds; nor can it be said, this body cannot be changed into a perfecter figure: But the meaning is, that that body consists of plane right lines; and this is always changeable into a perfecter figure, and yet can never reach to the perfection of a globe, although it always approaches nearer unto it; the case is the same in diverse degrees of life, which have indeed a beginning, but no end; so that the creature is always capable of a farther and perfecter degree of life, ad infinitum, and yet can never attain to be equal with God; for he is still infinitely more perfect than a creature, in its highest elevation or perfection, even as a globe is the most perfect of all other figures, unto which none can approach.

And thus life and figure are distinct, but not contrary attributes of one and the same substance, and figure serves the operations of life, as we see in the body of man or beast, how the figure of the eye serves the sight; the figure of the ear, the hearing; the figure of the mouth, teeth, lips, and tongue, serve the speech; the figure of the hands and fingers serve to work; the figure of the feet to walk; and so the figures of all the other members have their use, and very much conduce to the vital operations, which the spirit performs in these members; Yea the figure of the whole body is more commodious for the proper operations of human life, than any other figure whatsoever is, or could be made; So that life and figure consist very well together in one body, or substance, where figure is an instrument of life, without which no vital operation can be performed.

Likewise, local and mechanical motion (i.e.) the carrying of body from place to place, is a manner or operation distinct from action or vital operation, although they are inseparable, so that a vital action can in no wise be without all local motion, because this is the instrument thereof. So the eye cannot see, unless light enter it, which is a motion and stirs up a vital action in the eye, which is seeing; and so in all other vital operations in the whole body. But an action of life is a far nobler and diviner manner of operation than local motion; and yet both agree to one substance, and consist well together; for as the eye receives the light into itself, from the object which it seeth from without; so also it sends the same light to the object, and in this spirit and life is a vital action, uniting the object and sight together.

Wherefore Hobbes, and all others who side with him, grievously err, whilst they teach that sense and knowledge is no other than a reaction of corporeal particles one upon another, where, by reaction, he means no other than local and mechanical motion. But indeed sense and knowledge is a thing far more noble and divine, than any local or mechanical motion of any particles whatsoever; for it is the motion or action of life, which uses the other as its instrument, whose service consists herein; that is, to stir up a vital action in the subject or percipient; and can like local motion be transmitted through diverse bodies, although very far distant asunder, which therefore are united, and that without any new transition of body or matter, *ex. gr.* a beam of wood of an exceeding great length, is moved by one extreme from the north to the south, the other extreme will necessarily be moved also; and the action is transmitted through the whole beam, without any particles of matter sent hither to promote motion, from one extreme to the other; because the beam itself is sufficient to transmit the said motion: After the same manner also, a vital action can proceed together with local motion from one thing to another, and that too at a great distance, where there is an apt and fit medium to transmit it, and here we may observe a kind of divine spirituality or subtlety in every motion, and so in every action of life, which no created body or substance is capable of, viz. by intrinsical presence, which (as before is proved) agrees to no created substance; and yet agrees to every motion or action whatsoever: For motion or action is not a certain matter or substance, but only a manner of its being; and therefore is intrinsically present in the subject, whereof there is a *modus,* or manner, and can pass from body to body, at a great distance, if it finds a fit medium to transmit it; and by how much the stronger the motion is, so much the farther it reacheth; so when a stone is cast into standing waters, it causes a motion every way from the center to the circumference, forming circles still greater and greater at a great distance, by how much longer the time is, till at length it vanishes from our sight; and then without doubt, it makes yet more invisible circles for a longer space of time, which our dull senses cannot apprehend, and this motion is transmitted from the center to the circumference, not conveyed thither by any body or substance, carrying this motion with it from the stone. And as the external light also, seeing it is an action or motion stirred up by some illuminate body, may be transmitted through glass, crystal, or any other transparent body, without any substance, body, or matter, conveyed from that illuminate body from whence the said action proceeded, not that I would deny that abundance of subtle matter continually flows from all illuminate bodies, so that the whole substance of a burning candle is spent in such emanations: And this hath in it that motion or action, which we call light; but this motion or action may be increased, v.g. by crystal, where those subtle emanations of bodies may be restrained, that they cannot pass out at least in such abundance, as may be sufficient to communicate the whole light: But seeing crystal (which doth so easily transmit the light) is so hard and solid, How can it receive so many bodies, and transmit them so easily through it, when other bodies, neither so hard nor solid, do let or resist it? for wood is neither so hard nor solid as crystal, and yet crystal is transparent, but wood not; and certainly wood is more porous than crystal, because it is less solid, and consequently the light doth not enter by the pores of the crystal, but through the very substance of it; and yet so as not to adhere to it, or make any turgescency or increase of quantity, but by a certain intrinsic presence, because it is not a body or substance, but a mere action or motion. Now crystal is a fitter medium to receive this motion, which we call light, than wood is; and hence it is, that it pervades or passeth through that and not this; and as there is a great diversity of the motion and operation of bodies, so every motion requires its proper medium to transmit the same. Therefore 'tis manifest, that motion may be transmitted through diverse bodies, by another kind of penetration, than any body or matter (how subtle soever it be) is able to make; to wit, by intrinsic presence. And if mere local or mechanical motion can do that, then certainly a vital action (which is a nobler kind of motion) can do the same; and if it can penetrate those bodies, it passeth through by intrinsic presence, then it may in one moment be transmitted from one body to another, or rather require no time at all, I mean motion or action itself requires not the least time for its transmission, although 'tis impossible but that the body, wherein the motion is carried from place to place, ought to have some time, either greater or lesser, according to the quality of body and vehemency of motion which carries it.

And therefore we see how every motion and action, considered in the abstract, hath a wonderful subtlety or spirituality in it, beyond all created substances whatsoever, so that neither time nor place can limit the same; and yet they are nothing else but modes or manners of created substances viz. their strength, power and virtue, whereby they are extendible into great substances, beyond what the substance itself can make. And so we may distinguish extension into material and virtual, which twofold extension every creature hath; material extension is that which matter, body, or substance hath, as considered without all motion or action; and this extension (to speak properly) is neither greater or lesser, because it would still remain the same. A virtual extension is a motion or action which a creature hath, whether immediately given from God, or immediately received from its fellow creature. That which is immediately given of God (from whom also it hath its being,) and which is the natural and proper effect of its essence, is in a more proper way of speaking, a proper motion of the creature, proceeding from the innermost parts thereof; and therefore may be called internal motion, as distinguished from external, which is only from another; and therefore in respect thereof may be called foreign; and when the said external motion endeavors to carry a body, or any thing, to a place whereunto it hath properly no natural inclination, then it is preternatural and violent; as when a stone is thrown up into the air, which motion being preternatural and violent, is plainly local and mechanical, and no way vital, because it doth not proceed from the life of the thing so moved: But every motion, proceeding from the proper life and will of the creature, is vital; and this I call a motion of life, which is not plainly local and mechanical as the other, but hath in it a life, and vital virtue, and this is the virtual extension of a creature, which is either greater or lesser, according to that kind or degree of life wherewith the creature is endued, for when a creature arrives at a nobler kind and degree of life, then doth it receive the greater power and virtue to move itself, and transmit its vital motions to the greatest distance.

But how motion or action may be transmitted from one body to another, is with many a matter of great debate; because it is not a body or substance; and if it be only motion of body, how motion can pass properly with its own subject into another, because the very being of *modus* or manner, consist herein, viz. to exist or be inherent in its own body: The answer to this objection, which seemeth to me best, is this, that motion is not propagated from one body to another by local motion, because motion itself is not moved, but only moves the body in which it is; for if motion could be propagated by local motion, this motion would be propagated of another, and this again of another, and so ad infinitum which is absurd. Therefore the manner of the said propagation is (as it were) by real production or creation; so that as God and Christ can only create the substance of a thing, when as no creature can create or give being to any substance, no not as an instrument; so a creature, not of itself, but in subordination to God, as his instrument may give existence to motion and vital action, and so the motion in one creature may produce motion in another: And this is all a creature can do towards the moving itself or its fellow creatures, as being the instrument of God, by which motions a new substance is not created, but only new species of things, so that creatures may be multiplied in their kinds, whilst one acts upon, and moves another; and this is the whole work of the creature, or creation, as the instrument of God; but if it moves against his will, whose instrument it is, then it sins, and is punished for it: But God (as before was said) is not the cause of sin; for when a creature sins, he abuseth the power God hath granted him; and so the creature is culpable, and God entirely free from every spot or blemish hereof. If therefore we apply those things which have been already spoken, concerning the attributes of a body, viz. that it hath not only quantity and figure, but life also; and is not only locally and mechanically but vitally moveable, and can transmit its vital action whithersoever it pleaseth, provided it hath a medium aptly disposed, and if it hath none it can extend itself by the subtle emanation of its parts, which is the fittest and most proper medium of it, to receive and transmit its vital action. Hereby it will be easy to answer to all the arguments; whereby some endeavor to prove that a body is altogether uncapable of sense and knowledge; and it may be easily demonstrated, after what manner some certain body may gradually advance to that perfection, as not only to be capable of such sense and knowledge as brutes have, but of any kind of perfection whatsoever may happen in any man or angel; and so we may be able to understand the words of Christ, that of stones God is able to raise up children to Abraham, without flying to some strained metaphor; and if any one should deny this omnipotence of God, viz. that God is able of stones to raise up children to Abraham; that certainly would be the greatest presumption.

Damaris Cudworth, Lady Masham

DAMARIS CUDWORTH, LADY MASHAM, was born on January 18, 1659, and died on April 20, 1708. She was the daughter of the Cambridge Platonist, Ralph Cudworth. Although little is known of her education, she seems to have been brought up to be familiar with the work of her father and his colleagues, although she was not taught Latin, a language she learned in later life when she taught it to her son. She did, however, read French. In 1685, she married Sir Francis Masham, a landowner and the father of eight children by a previous marriage. By him, she became the mother of a son, Francis Cudworth Masham. The relationship that seems to have been of the greatest importance to her, however, was with John Locke, whom she first met while still unmarried at the age of twenty-three, probably at the home of their mutual friend, Edward Clarke. There are a number of her letters remaining from their correspondence, which flourished until Locke returned to England from Holland in 1688, after which their more frequent meetings put an end to their correspondence. Lady Masham prevailed upon Locke to first make lengthy visits to Oates, her country home, and eventually to take up permanent residence there, where he remained until his death in 1704. Locke interested himself in the education and upbringing of Masham's son, leaving him half his estate upon his death, but there is, unfortunately, little written record of the life of this household. Lady Masham survived Locke by only four years, and lies buried in Bath Abbey.

Masham's written output consists of about forty letters to Locke, which are largely personal in content; two published treatises, *A Discourse Concerning the Love of God* (1690) and *Occasional Thoughts in Reference to a Virtuous or Christian Life* (1705); and a brief but almost exclusively philosophical correspondence with Leibniz. Both treatises were published anonymously and both were attributed to Locke. (It should be noted that several of Locke's works were originally published anonymously; anonymous publication was not confined to women.) In the first treatise, Masham takes issue with several of the works of John Norris, a disciple of Malebranche, including the *Letters Concerning the Love of God*, his correspondence with Mary Astell. Masham argues against Norris's claim that God is the only cause and proper object of our love, on Lockean grounds, maintaining that our love for God derives from our sensory ideas of his creation. The second treatise argues for the importance of rationally grounded moral conduct in our religious life, and is interesting for the way in which she uses this claim as a step in an argument for the importance of education for women, to aid them in their religious duty and as a support for their role as mothers. Masham's arguments for the education of women can be interestingly compared with those of her currently better known contemporary, Mary Astell.

Masham's correspondence with Leibniz consists of an exchange of twelve letters, he writing to her in French and she replying in English. I have not included Leibniz's letters in this selection, but will summarize their contents briefly. Leibniz initiates the correspondence by thanking Masham for the copy of her father's book, which she had sent him and, as a source of his own views, recommending Bayle's summary. In the third letter, Leibniz lays out an account of his theory of what Masham refers to as simple beings, an account that Masham summarizes in her reply. In the fifth letter, Leibniz makes a number of points. He defends his hypothesis of preestablished harmony as not only possible but true, because it is superior to all others available, and the only one under which things can be understood to take place naturally and not miraculously. It is this preference for the natural over the miraculous, he explains, that leads him to say that it is not matter that thinks, but rather a simple, independent being joined to matter. He agrees with Masham that there are no created unextended substances, but resists the suggestion that this is because we cannot have the idea of an unextended substance, arguing that mathematicians can reason about things they cannot imagine. Leibniz deals with these issues again in his seventh letter, warning Masham against the kind of skepticism that can be engendered when we say the ways of God pass human understanding. He points out that we still know what fails to conform to God's nature, otherwise this would be like saying that divine justice passes human understanding, and concluding that God has committed tyrannical acts. In this reply, he also refuses to be drawn into a discussion of liberty, referring Masham to Locke. In a note, sent after this long reply, Leibniz asks Masham to inform him about Locke's claim (in *Essay* 4.10) that it is more difficult to make spirits than matter, which Leibniz says he takes to be of fundamental importance. In his tenth letter, after telling Masham of the death of Queen Sophie of Prussia and condoling with her on the death of Locke, Leibniz returns to the subject of Masham's father, Cudworth, and lists a great variety of areas of agreement between him and Cudworth, claiming that in holding that plastic force is itself mechanical, he is only explaining what Cudworth left unexplained. Masham's letters to Leibniz show what a person whose primary philosophical influence is Lockean makes of Leibniz's views.

❖ Selections from her
Correspondence with Leibniz

II

LADY MASHAM TO LEIBNIZ

Oates 29 March 1704

Though I am not in the number of those who can confirm
the advantageous idea you have of English ladies, yet I have been
too much conversant amongst learned men not to have contracted (so far as I am capable of it) a just value for them, or to
have been ignorant of the rank you hold in the commonwealth
of letters. This has disposed me long since to entertain with
pleasure any occasion of testifying a great respect for you, and
has lately suggested to me that my father's intellectual system
might possibly not be unacceptable to you. The esteem you express for that work pleases me very much both on this account,
and also as it is a new confirmation to me of the worth of that
performance.

I should be glad to have a farther view into the intellectual
world; and would therefore willingly have right conceptions of
the system you propose. To this purpose upon the receipt of
your obliging letter, I looked into the article of Rorarius in the
first edition of Mr. Bayle's *Dictionary* (not having the second by
me) and being by his quotation of you there, directed to the
Journal des Savans 1695, I read what is there published of it.
Perhaps my not being accustomed to such abstract speculations
made me not well comprehend what you say there of *forms*,
upon which I think you build your hypothesis: for (as it seems
to me) you sometimes call them *forces primitives*, sometimes *des
ames* sometimes *forms constitutives des substances*, and sometimes substances themselves; but such yet as are neither spirit,

---

Selections from Letters to Leibniz in C. I. Gerhardt, ed., *Die Philosophischen
Schriften von Leibniz*, vol. 3 (Berlin: 1975–1990), 337–338, 348–352, 358–361,
364–366, 369–373.

nor matter, whence I confess I have no clear idea of what you call *forms.*

That a man whose correspondence is so highly esteemed as yours by all the learned men of Europe should employ any of his valuable moments in the instruction of an ignorant woman is what I should not perhaps presume to importune you for, if your character was known to me only as a learned man; for those who are far advanced in learned studies, and high speculations may think themselves excused from such a condescension, but you I am confident would not condemn the most ignorant lover of truth; were I not secured by my sex of a favorable distinction from the obliging civility of a man conversant in courts. I take the liberty therefore to request the favor of you that you will by some explication or definition of them help me to conceive what your *forms* are; for I cannot but desire to understand a system recommended to me not only by the eminence of its author, but particularly also as tending to in large our idea of the divine perfections and the beauty of his works. If you please to add in short the sum of your answers to Mr. Bayle's objections in his second edition of his *Dictionary* it will be an additional obligation in giving me still further light into this matter.

I have ordered my father's discourse concerning the Lord's Supper to be sent you together with his intellectual system in the same vol: the value you express for the author makes me think you will not dislike to look into anything of his and though this treatise was writ when he was a young man, yet it was highly commended by our famous Selden. You will much oblige me in accepting of this book as from one who is with great esteem and respect etc.

Mr. Locke whose company I am so happy as to enjoy in my family, desires me to present you his humble service.

IV

LADY MASHAM TO LEIBNIZ

Oates 3 June 1704

Your great civility obliges me not the less for having presumed from your goodness upon more than I had any right to pretend to when I requested you would give yourself the pains of informing me farther concerning your hypothesis. To a mind possessed in any measure with a due admiration of the works of God nothing is more grateful than by farther discoveries therein of his divine perfections, to be sensibly engaged to adore that being which reason pronounces ought to be the supreme object of our affections.

An hypothesis thought by yourself and others conducing to such an end as this, could not but excite my enquiry; and it did so the more because that in reading what you have published, it seemed to myself also you had views there in which gave a very becoming idea of the wisdom of God in his works. The letter you have favored me with confirms me in this thought: but that I may be sure of having a certain and clear knowledge of your hypothesis permit me to tell you what I conceive it to be; in hopes you will rectify my mistakes if I am in any; which is what may easily happen to one so little conversant as I am in such speculations.

You take for granted that there is a simple being in us endued with action and perception. The same you say, differing only in the manner of perception, is in matter everywhere. That that simple being in us, which is called soul is distinguished from that of beasts (and yet more from that of other bodies about us) by the power of abstraction and framing thereby universal ideas. All these simple beings you think have; always will have; and ever since they existed have had organic bodies, proportioned to their perception. So that not only after death the soul does remain: but even the animal also. Generation and death, being but a displaying or concealment of these beings to, or from our view. The same principle of uniformity in the works of nature which has led you to believe this has you say, led you also to your system of the harmony preestablished between substances the which I thus understand.

Any action of the soul upon matter, or of matter upon the soul is inconceivable: these two have their laws distinct. Bodies follow the laws of mechanism and have a tendency to change *suivant les forces mouvantes*. Souls produce in themselves internal actions and have a tendency to change according to the perception that they have of good or ill. Now soul and body following each their proper laws, and neither of them acting thereby upon or affecting the other, such effects are yet produced from a harmony preestablished betwixt these substances, as if there was a real communication between them. So that the body acting constantly by its own laws of mechanism without receiving any variation or change therein from any action of the soul does yet always correspond to the passions and perceptions which the soul hath. And the soul in like manner, though not operated upon by the motions of matter, has yet at the same time that the body acts according to its laws of mechanism, certain perceptions or modifications which fail not to answer thereunto.

This is what I conceive you to say; in which (to tell you thoughts as insignificant as mine) I see nothing, peculiar, which seems not possible. I find a uniformity in it which pleases me: and the advantages proposed from this hypothesis are very desirable. But it appears not yet to me that this is more than a hypothesis; for as God's ways are not limited by our conceptions; the unintelligibleness or inconceivableness by us of any body but one, does not methinks, much induce a belief of that, being the way which God has chosen to make use of. Yet such an inference as this from our ignorance, I remember Malebranche (or some other assertor of an hypothesis) would make in behalf of occasional causes: to which hypothesis, amongst other exceptions, I think there is one, which I cannot without your help see, but that yours is a like liable to and that is from the organization of the body, wherein all that nice curiosity that is discoverable seeming useless, becomes superfluous and lost labor. To this difficulty likewise let me add that I conceive not why organism should be or can be thought, as you say is, essential to matter.

But these enquiries or other that might it may be on further thoughts occur to me, are less pertinent for me to make, than such a one as is more fundamental, although it does not peculiarly respect your hypothesis. Forms, explained by you to signify simple beings you elsewhere call *atomes de substance* and *forces primitives*, the nature whereof may, in another place say, you find to consist in force.

Force I presume cannot be the essence of any substance, but is the attribute of what you call a form, soul or *atome de substance*, of the essence whereof I find no positive idea, and your negation of their having any dimensions, makes their existence I confess inconceivable to me; as not being able to conceive an existence of that which is nowhere. If the locality of these substances were accounted for by their being as you (say) they are always in organized bodies, then they are somewhere: but if these *atomes de substance* are somewhere then they must have some extension, which you deny of them, who, I think, also place the union of the soul with its respective body in nothing else but that correspondence or conformity whereby in virtue of a preestablished harmony; souls and bodies acting a part, each by their own laws, the same effects are produced as if there was a real communication betwixt them. Though whether or no I perfectly comprehend your meaning in this part I am in doubt.

What I have here said I think enough for me to venture to trouble you with at once: and it will perhaps be more than enough to show you that you have judged by much too favorably of my apprehension. For I remember my father as well as other assertors of unextended substance to have said: That it is an imposition of imagination upon their reason in those who cannot be convinced of the reality of substances unextended.

So great authority as his was to me could not hinder me, if this be so, from being always under such an influence of imagination; which is what would not willingly be in any case. But wherever I have no idea of a thing; or demonstration of the truth of any proposition, the truth of which is inconceivable by me, I cannot and conclude, that I ought not to assent to what is asserted of either: since should I once do this I know not where I should stop; what should be the boundaries of assent. Or why I might not believe alike one thing as well as another.

Mr. Locke presents you his humble service and desires me to tell you he takes himself to be mightily obliged to you for your great civility expressed to him; in which he finds you a master as well as in philosophy and everything else. His want of health he says now, and the little remains he counts he has of life, has put an end, to his enquiries into philosophical speculations. Though if he were still in the heat of that pursuit he could not be so ignorant of you or himself as to take upon him to be the judge of what you have well considered: much less to be the instructor of a man of your known extraordinary parts and merit. He takes it for a great honor done him, that you have condescended to read and consider, as you say, his essay upon the understanding and that you think it worth the while by your larger views to remove some difficulties, and supply some defects that are therein. This if he had any other end in publishing that treatise but some small service to truth and knowledge would flatter his vanity. That it would be preserved to posterity by the touches of so great a master: by whose hand it would be redeemed from some of its own imperfections. All Mr. Locke's friends have at present the grief to apprehend that they shall enjoy the happiness of his friendship but a little time; the infirmity of ill lungs daily increasing upon him, in an age that is considerable.

I am much pleased sir to have made you a present, that is both acceptable to you, and that can possibly contribute anything to your enriching the world by the effects of your meditations. If you shall think me worthy of your instruction, or at any time of any communication of your thoughts I shall always (as I ought to do) look upon it as condescension in you which will oblige me to be with the greatest acknowledgment as well as esteem etc.

VI

LADY MASHAM TO LEIBNIZ

Oates 8 August 1704

Whatever allowances are to be made for the language of civility to ladies, differing but little from what would look like flattery to one of your own sex; yet I find a pleasure in being praised by you, which I justify to myself from a belief that when you honor me with such expressions of your good opinion, you make me the best return in your power for that well grounded esteem I have for you, by a desire which that has created in you of finding me worthy of yours. Nor shall I ever reckon it a small matter if I have desert enough to engage those of a distinguished merit to wish that I had more. Thus, if I do flatter myself, I am by a vanity but very little moderated, or rather refined beyond that of others, pleased with the favorable things you say of me, without that cruel allay attending this satisfaction which a consciousness of not resembling the picture you have made for me must otherwise give me.

Whether I have rightly represented your system you best can tell: and what you say on that subject I am proud of; whilst the inferences you would draw from thence to my advantage can give me only a due acknowledgment for your wishing me so much fitter for your correspondence than I am. But however justly I may have expressed your sense so far as I endeavored to represent it, your answers to some of my enquiries makes me question whether I fully apprehended all that is included in your hypothesis. For I do not yet sufficiently see upon what you ground organism's being essential to matter: or indeed very well understand your meaning in these words that organism is not absolutely essential to matter but to matter *arrangée par une sagesse souveraine*. What you would build upon this, forms a very transcendent conception of the divine artifice; and such as I think could only occur to the thoughts of one possessed with the highest admiration of the wisdom of his maker: but if you infer the truth of this notion only from its being the most agreeable one that you can frame to that attribute of God, this singly seems to me not to be concluding. Since we can in my opinion only infer from thence that whatsoever God does must be according to infinite wisdom: but are not able with our short and narrow views to determine what the operations of an infinitely wise being must be.

The principle of action called by you *force primitive* is you say a substance: of the which, I still perceive not the positive idea perception being but the action of this substance: what you add concerning its perceptions, in these words, *suivant l'analogie qu'elle doit avoir avec notre ame*, makes me again believe that I do not fully understand your scheme: since I thought before that the soul this *force primitive*, or principle of action, had been the same thing. You say *refermer les ames dans les dimensions c'est vouloir imaginer les ames comme des corps*. In regard of extension this is true; and extension is to me, inseparable from the notion of all substance. I am yet sensible that we ought not to reject truths because they are not imaginable by us (where there is ground to admit them). But truth being but the attributing certain affections conceived to belong to the subject in question. I can by no means attribute anything to a subject whereof I have no conception at all; as I am conscious to myself I have not of unextended substance. What you instance in therefore of lines incommensurable seems not to me to answer the case; for I herein do conceive the proposition, and have clear ideas of lines incommensurable, though I do not see the reason of their incommensurability: but of an unextended substance I have not any conception, from whence I can affirm or deny anything concerning it.

Why you think that there is no created substance complete without extension: or that the soul (which you suppose a distinct substance) would without the body be a substance incomplete without extention, I understand not: but my own belief that there is no substance whatever unextended is (as I have already said), grounded upon this that I have no conception of such a thing. I cannot yet but conceive two very different substances to be in the universe, though extension alike agrees to them both. For I clearly conceive an extension without solidity, and a solid extension: to some system of which last if it should be affirmed that God did annex thought, I see no absurdity in this from there being nothing in extension and impenetrability or solidity, from whence thought can naturally, or by a train of causes be derived; the which I believe to be demonstrable it cannot be. But that was never supposed by me; and my question in the case would be this; whether God could not as conceivably by us as create an unextended substance, and then unite it to an extended substance (wherein, by the way, there is methinks on your side two difficulties for one) whether God, I say, could not as conceivably by us as his doing this would be, add (if he so pleased) the power of thinking to that substance which has solidity. Solidity and thought being both of them but attributes of some unknown substance and I see not why it may not be one and the same which is the common support of both these; there appearing to me no contradiction in a so existence of thought and solidity in the same substance. Neither can apprehend it to be more inexplicable that God should give thought to a substance which I know not, but whereof I know some of its attributes, than to another, supposed, substance of whose very being I have no conception at all, and that any substance whatsoever should have thought belonging to it, or resulting from it, otherwise than as God has willed it shall have so, I cannot apprehend.

That God does in framing and ordering of all his works always make use of the most simple means I doubt not, this appearing to me most suitable to his wisdom, but whether or no, these simple means or methods are always such as surpass not a created intelligence, I do not know: but am very apt to believe that God's ways are past our finding out, in this sense.

I have no sooner scribbled to you these thoughts of mine, than I fear wearying you by my dullness. I shall therefore wave taking notice of anything more that has occurred to me in considering the several parts of your letter; or making any such farther inquiries as perhaps were there resolved, I might be able in some measure to clear to myself. I will however now mention to you one difficulty (as I conceive) in your hypothesis, which I think not that I could ever extricate it from without your assistance and it is to me a very material one. Viz how to reconcile your system to liberty or free agency: for though in regard of any compulsion from other causes, we are according thereto free, yet I see not how we can be so in respect of the first mover. This I omitted taking notice of in my last not only because I thought it too remote an inquiry for one who wanted to be enlightened concerning the very foundation you built upon: but also because I must acknowledge that I cannot make out liberty either with or without any hypothesis whatsoever. Though as being persuaded that I feel myself a free agent and that freedom to act is necessary to our being accountable for our actions, I not only conclude we are endued therewith, but am very tenacious hereof: whence I should be sorry to find from any new hypothesis new difficulties in maintaining of this. I think not much that I need seek to justify to you the part which I own my inclination has in this opinion; since what you have said in print persuades me that you have the same belief with the same bias. I might else perhaps, allege (in my excuse at least) that as I am a true English woman, I cannot but naturally have a passion for liberty in all senses wherein I consider it: and I would not have so much as the philosophy of Hanover unfavorable to any kind of it.

What you write on the subject of Mr. Locke's health, he is much obliged by: and I am no less so when you recommend to me the care of one of the best friends, I have in the world as a matter in which you interest yourself. If I could contribute to the prolonging so valuable a life as his, I should think this one of the best uses I could ever make of my own. He is not only still with me, but in all probability will never have health enough to permit him the thoughts of leaving anymore a place which he has made agreeable to others by having for many years chosen to spend therein a great part of his time. Rational conversation with mutual good will, has the greatest charms that I know in life, and I have hitherto been very happy in respect of that enjoyment. To my felicity in which kind I think it a considerable addition to be honored with your correspondence at such a distance, and that I am allowed to assure you of my being with great esteem etc.

IX

LADY MASHAM TO LEIBNIZ

Oates 24 November, 1704

It being a long while since the date of your first letter to me, though not very long since I received it; the high value that I have for the honor of your correspondence makes me fear incurring the suspicion of a neglect I can never be guilty of in your regard; and induces me now to write, though the loss I have but lately had; and since that the solicitous care which attends the first sending an only child into the world under his own conduct, does at present much indispose me.

Yours of the 16th of September came not to my hands till our 31 of October: the day wherein was performed the last office to one that had been my friend above half my lifetime. Mr. Locke I mean. A friend who though very accidentally an equal infance and perfectly unknown to my family, has supplied to me the plan of a father and brother: and to whose direction, next to the favor of God, I chiefly ascribe it if my son, (as I have reason to hope) be blessed with a sound mind in a sound body. But this has been but the best effect of Mr. Locke's friendship, not the only one: for he has in his last will left to my son (or in case of his death to myself) a legacy in money of a value seldom given by any to such as are no way related: with other gifts to him amongst which is the division of his library betwixt him, and his kinsman and executor Mr. Peter King; a man of great worth on many accounts and particularly as a member of parliament (wherein no one is believed more immoveably true to the Protestant interest).

In telling you these obligations which I have had to Mr. Locke, I shall (I hope) make my excuse, if the tribute which I pay of a well merited affection to the memory of this extraordinary friend, as well as extraordinary man, unfits me yet for other thought than such as the heart dictates.

Your second letter came to my hands but two days since. I have no remembrance of it at present if Mr. Locke has ever explained to me his thoughts concerning the production of matter. That this is left inconceivable than the creation of an immaterial substance was what I imagined before I knew Mr. Locke, which has made me perhaps, more inadvertent than I should else have been to what he intimates in the chapter you cite.

Not long since, the library keeper of the University of Oxford desired of Mr. Locke, for the Bodleian Library, the books of which he was the author. Mr. Locke in return to this request, presented to the said library all the books published under his name. But in a codicil to his will he takes notice that he had not been herein understood fully to have answered the request made him; it being supposed he was the author of other treatises to which his name was not prefixed. In compliance therefore (he says) with what was desired in the utmost extent of it, and in acknowledgement of the honor done him in thinking his writings, worthy to be placed amongst the works of the learned, in that august repository; he does further give to the public library of the University of Oxford these following books, which are; *three letters Concerning Toleration. Two Treatises of Government. The Reasonableness of Christianity as delivered in the scriptures. A Vindication of the Reasonableness etc. from Mr. Edwards Re-*

flections. A 2d vindication of the Reasonableness of Christianity. These he says are all the books whereof he was the author, published without his name, and many other anonymous books besides these, having been attributed to Mr. Locke. I thought you might not be unwilling to know what he truly did write, and what was not his; which has made me transcribe this so solemn a declaration. If you have read the *Reasonableness of Christianity* as delivered in the scriptures, I should be very glad to know your thoughts of it. If you have not seen this book, I desire to present you with it. It was long ago translated into French by a person whom I have been happy in having for preceptor to my son, Monsr. Coste, the translator of Mr. Locke's *Essay*.

I am much obliged to you sir for your good wishes. They will always be a pleasure to, and always returned by your most humble servant etc.

XI

LADY MASHAM TO LEIBNIZ

Oates 20 October 1705

I should have no cause to wonder if you were not unwilling to give over a commerce which brought you so poor returns as are my letters for yours. Your excusing to me therefore your silence is very obliging as a mark of your putting a value on my correspondence that it has no claim to: but the reason you give of your not having writ to me sooner has renewed in me a sorrow which I could not but partake in with all the world to whom were known (though but by fame only) the great endowments and accomplishments of that admirable princess whose death has so much afflicted you. One cannot have a deeper sense than I have of your particular loss in this universal one: and if ever grief was just yours must be allowed to be so.

The experience of the wisest does I find on some occasions attest to this truth, that *La sensibilité ne depend pas du raisonnement.* There is however much difference betwixt them and others; in that if their reason does not always triumph, it yet at least hinders passion from doing so: and it is a happy distinction not to be led captive by those tyrants under which the generality of mankind suffer a worse slavery than the most arbitrary masters can inflict.

I was highly honored in having any thoughts of mine communicated to the queen of Prussia: but what you thought worth the answering I cannot wonder that she vouchsafed a hearing to.

I have flattered myself since my last to you that possibly, within another year I might have the opportunity to converse with you better than by letters, in seeing you at Hanover: for if some whose judgments I rely upon, had thought it fit for a young gentleman destined to the study of the law to spend a little time first in traveling, I should with his father's leave, gladly have accompanied my son in such a voyage: both as proposing great pleasure therein; and also as having been persuaded that traveling would contribute to my health, which has been much disordered this last year.

You have added to the many reasons I have to regret the death of Mr. Locke in letting me know that it will hinder the public from profiting by your remarks upon his *Essay*. The debates of those who equally search truth cannot but be advantageous to the discovery of it or to the setting it in a clearer light: and whichever it be, both parties in such cases will think themselves alike gainers.

I am sorry with you that the strength or weakness of any notion which you believe important to be known, should not be so. It were to be wished that all who in respect of any useful truth, have views beyond others would not neglect to communicate them, that so they may be out of danger of being useless to the world. This should methinks induce you to oblige, as Mr. Le Clerc tells you you would do, all the lovers of philosophy, in explaining at large your system; whereby it being set in a just light, the advantages of it may neither be lost; nor prejudiced, by the unskillful representation that, it may be, some other person who shall less perfectly comprehend it may some time or other, venture to give of it. This I cannot but wish; and this I find some hope you will be, excited to by Mr. Bayle's reflection upon your sentiments amongst those of others.

If you have read what has been writ betwixt him and Mr. Le Clerc on the subject of the hypothesis of the plastic nature as asserted by my father, I should be very glad to know whether what Mr. Bayle has offered does amount to anything more than a begging of the question. That God cannot make an unknowing agent so as to act to wise ends; yet without such his perpetual direction thereof as the Cartesian hypothesis gives to material causes: for if it be conceivable for God to do so, but not conceivable for senseless matter of itself to act for ends; my father's hypothesis is methinks sufficiently secured from the retorsion of atheists, without being in the same case with anyone which makes God the immediate efficient cause of all the effects of nature. Since my father does not therein assert (as Mr. Bayle says he does) that God has been able to give to creatures a faculty of producing excellent works, (viz such as is the organization of plants and animals) separate from all knowledge etc.: but only a faculty of executing instrumentally his ideas or designs, in the production of such excellent works: so that (according to him) there is (differently from what Mr. Bayle asserts of his hypothesis) an inseparable union betwixt the power of producing excellent works, and the idea of their essence and manner of producing them: and it seems to me that there can be no pretense for the retorsion of atheists unless it were asserted, that God had been able to give to creatures a faculty of producing excellent works, the ideas whereof never were in any understanding: but my father is so far from asserting any such thing as this, that he holds the operations of the plastic nature to be essentially and necessarily dependent on the ideas in the divine intellect. So that (I conceive) if matter could be supposed to have of itself that same power which plastic natures are said to have by the gift of God, it would not help the atheist's cause at all: because the power given to plastic nature's being only a power to execute the ideas of a perfect mind; if there were no mind in the universe; this power in the matter must lie forever dormant and unproductive, of any such excellent work as is spoken of.

Thus I see not in my father's hypothesis that there is effectively (as Mr. Bayle affirms) a compatibility supposed of a power to organize animals, with the want of knowledge. Since to the production of such a work as this, two things (according to my father) must concur viz the idea of the work to be executed, with an executive power of bringing this idea into real existence: and it is only the last of these which he ascribes to plastic natures.

But Mr. Bayle argues, that if plastic natures have no entire efficiency of their own, they will then need such perpetual direction as is ascribed to material causes; and so my father's hypothesis will be but in the same case with the Cartesian. Mr. Bayle affirms this; but (as I think) he nowhere proves it: all that he offers amounting (as I have already observed) only to a begging of this question, that God cannot make a creature to act but either from ideas of what it does; or else by such perpetual direction as that of the Cartesian material causes. Whence he rightly infers that if plastic natures act not by ideas which they have, as it is presumed the Destroying Angel did to in distinguishing the Egyptians from the Israelites etc. they then must act as he supposes fire, had it so pleased God, might have done, in destroying the first born of Egypt; viz by God's perpetual applying and directing it.

But to anyone's bare assertion that a thing is inconceivable, it is surely answer sufficient that others find it not to be so. Though my father has given some instances which he thinks prove the possibility of such a manner of action as he ascribes to plastic natures; viz in the operations of habits: as (for example) those of singing and dancing: which shall oftentimes direct the motions of the body, or voice, without any consideration of what the next note, or motion should be.

I beg leave here to trespass so much farther on your patience, as to observe to you one thing wherein Mr. Bayle is mistaken in reference to this matter, which has not been taken notice of, and that is, in a presuming that my father designed in introducing his hypothesis, to oppose the modern Cartesians: whereas he (not understanding French) did not know that the modern Cartesians differed so much from their master as to hold that God was the immediate efficient cause of all the effects of nature. And the hypothesis of the plastic nature (produced by him for the acquitting from the suspicion of atheism some who held a plastic life distinct from the animal) was very far from having the Cartesians in view; however they may find themselves convinced when the opinion of such is condemned as held that God himself did all immediately in the efformation and organization of the bodies of animals, as well as the other phenomena: which with the opinion of all things coming to pass fortuitously, my father considered as the only two hypothesis, which were opposed to that of plastic natures.

Now Mr. Bayle considering perpetual direction only in such a sense as makes God the immediate efficient cause of all the effects of nature, presumes that my father is obliged to deny all kind of perpetual direction to plastic natures, which (as I take it) he does not: since (according to him) their operations are always determined by the ideas in the divine intellect; and his hypothesis opposes only such direction as makes God the immediate efficient cause of all the works of nature. Plastic natures being by him substituted as the agents or executioners of the divine will and pleasure. As perpetual direction then is understood, or may be explained, it seems to me that plastic natures may be, and are by my father in what he says of them, both affirmed and denied to have perpetual direction: in which, if he talks contradictiously or inconsistently it lies upon Mr. Bayle to show that he does so, stating first rightly what is herein asserted by him.

I pretend not at all to be positive in anything which I have here ventured to say on so nice a subject, and so much above my examination as not easily to be set in a due light by two so acute and extraordinary men as both Mr. Le Clerc and Mr. Bayle are. I only take the liberty briefly to suggest to you my thoughts thereon to the end that I may learn from you how far they are right.

The last answer of Mr. Le Clerc I have not yet read, his civility in sending me one (which I hear has miscarried) having made me thus long neglect buying it. But I am told that Mr. Bayle will still reply: and that the subject of the controversy is by some thought to be by Mr. Le Clerc's answer too much enlarged in a consideration of the usefulness of the hypothesis of plastic natures, which is not necessary to the inquiry whether or no, this hypothesis is exposed to the retorsion of atheists.

On which subject I have dwelt long enough both to need your pardon and to forbid my adding anything more to this letter that might induce you to explain to me farther your sentiments on some other important inquiries mentioned in the last letter you honored me with. I am with due acknowledgment of your condescension in encouraging me in this manner to trouble you, and with very great esteem and respect etc.

Mary Astell

MARY ASTELL was born on November 12, 1666, in Newcastle-upon-Tyne. She came from a family of merchants, and so, although she grew up comfortably, she was not a member of the nobility like many of the other women writing philosophy in this period. Although she did acquire a considerable reputation for her writings during her lifetime, she lived quietly and privately and there is much about her life that remains unknown. Even some facts that are often repeated about her remain dubious. Her intelligence is said to have been recognized by an uncle who educated her, but the man who is identified as this uncle, a clergyman named Ralph Astell, died when Astell was thirteen, so the education he provided must have been at an early age. Astell's father died when she was twelve and her mother when she was eighteen. Two years later, surprisingly, she moved alone to London, but how she lived and how she supported herself remain unknown. She was put in touch with a bookseller who gave her work writing pamphlets. She was also befriended by several titled ladies living in Chelsea, where Astell settled, who may have provided her with financial support as well as friendship. She never married and lived a simple and pious life, dying on May 9, 1731, of breast cancer.

One thing that is remarkable about Mary Astell is the extent of her published writings. She not only published copiously, but on a variety of subjects, contributing to several of the religious and political controversies of her day. The work that has been recovered and for which she is known today are her "feminist" writings, *A Serious Proposal to the Ladies*, Parts I and II, and *Reflections on Marriage*. In the first she argues that women's shortcomings are due to lack of education and not to lack of native intellectual ability and argues for the importance of education for women in order to fit them rationally for their religious duty. To this end, Astell urged the establishment of institutions into which women could retreat, either to be educated or to live, if they remained unmarried. The argument in favor of education for women is continued in *Reflections on Marriage*, a more polemical work, in which Astell maintains that only a well-trained reason can allow women to avoid the pitfalls of a bad choice of marriage partner or help in dealing with the vicissitudes if a bad marriage is nevertheless entered into. Despite what seems like the radical nature of the views expressed in these works, Mary Astell chiefly allied herself with the most conservative elements of her day, the High Church Anglicans and Torys, against the Whigs, who had been responsible for redefining the relationship between the monarch and the people as a contract. She made several contributions to the debates raging at this time, *A Fair Way with Dissenters and their Patrons, Moderation Truly Stated*, and *An Impartial Enquiry into the Causes of Rebellion and Civil War in this Kingdom*, in which she argued in favor of the divine right of kings and against the practice of occasional conformity, in which those who did not wish to conform to the Anglican Church could worship there once a year and get a certificate that permitted them to hold public office. In Astell's other writings, she enters into discussion with various well-known philosophers of her day, largely over religious issues. She had a correspondence with Malebranche's English disciple, John Norris, over such issues as God's role in the causation of pain and sin and about our duty, as Norris conceived it, to love God only. Norris prevailed upon her to publish their correspondence, which came out in 1695, entitled *Letters Concerning the Love of God*. This volume occasioned Lady Masham's *Discourse Concerning the Love of God,* the Lockean nature of which led Astell to attribute it to Locke. She made it also the target of one of her last works, *The Christian Religion, as Professed by a Daughter of the Church of England,* along with Locke's *Reasonableness of Christianity* and his correspondence with Stillingfleet. This last work is a four-hundred-page treatise in which Astell lays out her religious philosophy and discusses at some length Locke's speculation that God could have superadded thought to matter. This in turn provoked Masham's *Occasional Thoughts.*

Part II of *A Serious Proposal to the Ladies,* from which this selection is taken, was published three years after the first part originally appeared, and contains Astell's account of the sort of education from which she had argued women would benefit. The ideas of Locke, Descartes, and Arnauld have variously been detected in it. Astell certainly quotes frequently from Arnauld's *Art of Thinking* and also from Descartes's *Principles,* but the work is far from being a compilation of the work of others. It provides an interesting example of how certain ways of thinking about the mind are in the air by the end of the seventeenth century, but the work is organized so as to allow Astell to make what she sees as important points about the nature of human knowledge and human cognitive faculties. Her concern is to link the development of our rational faculties with the practical action that is necessary for our salvation, so that she argues that we should develop the mind in the service of rational choice, and not for idle speculation. Thus, although she supposes humans to be unavoidably ignorant of many matters, what she takes to be important is that we avoid error by restraining the passions so that our will does not outrun our judgment.

✧ Selections from
A Serious Proposal to the Ladies, Part II

CHAP. III

Concerning the Improvement of the Understanding.

The perfection of the understanding consisting in the clearness and largeness of its view, it improves proportionably as its ideas become clearer and more extensive. But this is not so to be understood as if all sorts of notices contributed to our improvement, there are some things which make us no wiser when we know them, others which 'tis best to be ignorant of. But that understanding seems to me the most exalted, which has the clearest and most extensive view of such truths as are suitable to its capacity, and necessary or convenient to be known in this present state. For being that we are but creatures, our understanding in its greatest perfection has only a limited excellency. It has indeed a vast extent, and it were not amiss if we tarried a little in the contemplation of its powers and capacities, provided that the prospect did not make us giddy, that we remember from whom we have received them, and balance those lofty thoughts which a view of our intellectuals may occasion, with the depressing ones which the irregularity of our morals will suggest, and that we learn from this inspection, how indecorous it is to busy this bright side of us in mean things, seeing it is capable of such noble ones.

Selections from Mary Astell's *A Serious Proposal to the Ladies*, reprint of London: R. Wilken, 1697.

Human nature is indeed a wonderful composure admirable in its outward structure, but much more excellent in the beauties of its inward, and she who considers in whose image her soul was created, and whose blood was shed to redeem it, cannot prize it too much, nor forget to pay it her utmost regard. There's nothing in this material world to be compared to it, all the gay things we dote on, and for which we many times expose our souls to ruin, are of no consideration in respect of it. They are not the good of the soul, its happiness depends not on them, but they often deceive and withdraw it from its true good. It was made for the contemplation and enjoyment of its God, and all souls are capable of this though in a different degree and by measures somewhat different, as we hope will appear from that which follows.

Truth in general is the object of the understanding, but all truths are not equally evident, because of the limitation of the human mind, which though it can gradually take in many truths, yet cannot any more than our sight attend to many things at once: And likewise, because God has not thought fit to communicate such ideas to us as are necessary to the disquisition of some particular truths. For knowing nothing without us but by the idea we have of it, and judging only according to the relation we find between two or more ideas, when we cannot discover the truth we search after by intuition or the immediate comparison of two ideas, 'tis necessary that we should have a third by which to compare them. But if this middle idea be wanting, though we have sucient evidence of those two which we would compare, because we have a clear and distinct conception of them, yet we are ignorant of those truths which would arise from their comparison, because we want a third by which to compare them.

To give an instance of this in a point of great consequence, and of late very much controverted though to little purpose, because we take a wrong method, and would make that the object of science which is properly the object of faith, the doctrine of the trinity. Revelation which is but an exaltation and improvement of reason has told us, that the Father is God, the Son is God, and the Holy Ghost is God, and our idea of the godhead of any one of these persons, is as clear as our idea of any of the other. Both reason and revelation assure us that God is one simple essence, undivided, and infinite in all perfection, this is the natural idea which we have of God. How then can the Father be God, the Son God, and the Holy Ghost God, when yet there is but one God? That these two propositions are true we are certain, both because God who cannot lie has revealed them, and because we have as clear an idea of them as it is possible a finite mind should have of an infinite nature. But we cannot find out how this should be, by the bare comparison of these two ideas without the help of a third by which to compare them. This God has not thought fit to impart to us, the prospect it would have given us would have been too dazzling, too bright for mortality to bear, and we ought to acquiesce in the divine will. So then, we are well assured that these two propositions are true, There is but one God; and, there are three persons in the godhead: but we know not the manner how these things are. Nor can our acquiescence be thought unreasonable, nor the doctrine we subscribe to be run down as absurd and contradictory by every little warm disputer and pretender to reason, whose life is perhaps a continual contradiction to it, and he knows little of it besides the name. For we ought not to think it strange that God has folded up his own nature, not in darkness, but in an adorable and inaccessible light, since his wisdom sees it fit to keep us ignorant of our own. We know and feel the union between our soul and body, but who amongst us sees so clearly, as to find out with certitude and exactness, the secret ties which unite two such different substances, or how they are able to act upon each other? We are conscious of our own liberty, who ever denies it, denies that he is capable of rewards and punishments, degrades his nature and makes himself but a more curious piece of mechanism; and none but atheists will call in question the providence of God, or deny that he governs *all*, even the most free of all his creatures. But who can reconcile me these? Or adjust the limits between God's Prescience and man's free-will? Our understandings are sufficiently illuminated to lead us to the fountain of life and light, we do or may know enough to fill our souls with the noblest conceptions, the humblest adoration, and the

entirest love of the author of our being, and what can we desire
farther? If we make so ill a use of that knowledge which we have,
as to be so far puffed up with it, as to turn it against him who gave
it, how dangerous would it be for us to have more knowledge, in
a state in which we have so little humility! But if vain man will
pretend to wisdom, let him first learn to know the length of his
own line.

Though the human intellect has a large extent, yet being
limited as we have already said, this limitation is the cause of
those different modes of thinking, which for distinction sake we
call faith, science and opinion. For in this present and imperfect
state in which we know not any thing by intuition, or immediate view, except a few first principles which we call self-evident,
the most of our knowledge is acquired by reasoning and deduction: And these three modes of understanding, faith, science
and opinion are no otherwise distinguished than by the different degrees of clearness and evidence in the premises from
whence the conclusion is drawn.

Knowledge in a proper and restricted sense and as appropri-
ated to science, signifies that clear perception which is followed
by a firm assent to conclusions rightly drawn from premises of
which we have clear and distinct ideas. Which premises or principles must be so clear and evident, that supposing us reasonable
creatures, and free from prejudices and passions, (which for the
time they predominate as good as deprive us of our reason) we
cannot withhold our assent from them without manifest violence to our reason.

But if the nature of the thing be such as that it admits of no
undoubted premises to argue from, or at least we don't at present know of any, or that the conclusion does not so necessarily
follow as to give a perfect satisfaction to the mind and to free
it from all hesitation, that which we think of it is then called
opinion.

Again, if the medium we make use of to prove the proposition be authority, the conclusion which we draw from it is said
to be believed; This is what we call faith, and when the authority
is God's a divine faith.

Moral certainty is a species of knowledge whose proofs are

of a compounded nature, in part resembling those which belong to science, and partly those of faith. We do not make the whole process ourselves, but depend on another for the *immediate* proof, but we ourselves deduce the *mediate* from circumstances and principles as certain and almost as evident as those of science, and which lead us to the immediate proofs and make it unreasonable to doubt of them indeed we not seldom deceive ourselves in this manner, by inclining alternately to both extremes. Sometimes we reject truths which are morally certain as conjectural and probable only, because they have not a physical and mathematical certainty, which they are incapable of. At another time we embrace the slightest conjectures and anything that looks with probability, as moral certainties and real verities, if fancy, passion or interest recommend them; so ready are we to be determined by these rather than by solid reason.

In this enumeration of the several ways of knowing, I have not reckoned the senses, in regard that we're more properly said to be *conscious* of than to *know* such things as we perceive by sensation. And also because that light which we suppose to be let into our ideas by our senses is indeed very dim and fallacious, and not to be relied on till it has passed the test of reason; neither do I think there is any mode of knowledge which may not be reduced to those already mentioned.

Now though there's a great difference between opinion and science, true science being immutable but opinion variable and uncertain, yet there is not such a difference between faith and science as is usually supposed. The difference consists not in the certainty but in the way of proof; the objects of faith are as rationally and as firmly proved as the objects of science, though by another way. As science demonstrates things that are *seen*, so faith is the evidence of such as are *not seen*. And he who rejects the evidence of faith in such things as belong to its cognizance, is as unreasonable as he who denies propositions in geometry that are proved with mathematical exactness.

There's nothing true which is not in itself demonstrable, or which we should not pronounce to be true had we a clear and intuitive view of it. But as was said above we see very few things by intuition, neither are we furnished with mediums to make the process ourselves in demonstrating all truths, and therefore there are some truths which we must either be totally ignorant of, or else receive them on the testimony of another person, to whose understanding they are clear and manifest though not to ours. And if this person be one who can neither be deceived nor deceive, we're as certain of those conclusions which we prove by his authority, as we are of those we demonstrate by our own reason: nay more certain, by how much his reason is more comprehensive and infallible than our own.

Science is following the process ourselves upon clear and evident principles; faith is a dependence on the credit of another, in such matters as are out of our view. And when we have very good reason to submit to the testimony of the person we believe, faith is as firm, and those truths it discovers to us as truly intelligible, and as strongly proved in their kind as science.

In a word, as every sense so every capacity of the understanding has its proper object. The objects of science are things within our view, of which we may have clear and distinct ideas, and nothing should be determined here without clearness and evidence. To be able to repeat any person's dogma without forming a distinct idea of it ourselves, is not to know but to remember; and to have a confused indeterminate idea is to conjecture not to understand.

The objects of faith are as certain and as truly, intelligible in themselves as those of science, as has been said already, only we become persuaded of the truth of them by another method, we do not *see* them so clearly and distinctly as to be unable to disbelieve them. Faith has a mixture of the will that it may be rewardable, for who will thank us for giving our assent where it was impossible to withold it? Faith then may be said to be a sort of knowledge capable of reward, and men are infidels not for want of conviction, but through an *unwillingness* to believe.

But as it is a fault to believe in matters of science, where we may expect demonstration and evidence, so it is a reproach to our understanding and a proof of our disingenuity, to require that sort of process peculiar to science, for the confirmation of such truths as are not the proper objects of it. It is as ridiculous as to reject music, because we cannot taste or smell it, or to deny there is such a thing as beauty because we do not hear it. He who would see with his ears and hear with his eyes may indeed set up in *Bedlam* for a man of an extraordinary reach, a sagacious person who won't be imposed on, one who must have more authentic proofs than his dull forefathers were content with. But men of dry reason and a moderate genius, I suppose will think nature has done very well in allotting to each sense its proper employment, and such as these will as readily acknowledge that it is as honorable for the soul to believe what is truly the object of faith, as it is for her to know what is really the object of her knowledge. And were we not strangely perverse we should not scruple divine authority when we daily submit to human. Whoever has not seen Paris has nothing but human authority to assure him there is such a place, and yet he would be laughed at as ridiculous who should call it in question, though he may as well in this as in another case pretend that his informers have designs to serve, intend to impose on him and mock his credulity. Nay how many of us daily make that a matter of faith which indeed belongs to science, by adhering blindly to the dictates of some famous philosopher in physical truths, the principles of which we have as much right to examine, and to make deductions from them as he had?

To sum up all: we may know enough for all the purposes of life, enough to busy this active faculty of thinking, to employ and entertain the spare intervals of time and to keep us from rust and idleness, but we must not pretend to fathom all depths with our short line, we should be wise unto sobriety, and reckon that we know very little if we go about to make our *own* reason the standard of all truth. It is very certain that nothing is true but what is conformable to reason, that is to the divine reason of which ours is but a short faint ray, and it is as certain that there are many truths which human reason cannot comprehend. Therefore to be thoroughly sensible of the capacity of the mind, to discern precisely its bounds and limits and to direct our studies and inquiries accordingly, to know what is to be known, and to believe what is to be believed is the property of a wise person. To be content with too little knowledge, or to aspire to overmuch is equally a fault, to make that use of our understandings which God has fitted and designed them for is the medium which we ought to take. For the difference between a plowman and a doctor does not seem to me to consist in this, That the business of the one is to search after knowledge, and that the other has nothing to do with it. No, whoever has a rational soul ought surely to employ it about some truth or other, to procure for it right ideas, that its judgments may be true though its knowledge be not very extensive. But herein lies the difference, that though truth is the object of every individual understanding, yet all are not equally enlarged nor able to comprehend so much; and they whose capacities and circumstances of living do not fit them for it, lie not under that obligation of extending their view which persons of a larger reach and greater leisure do. There is indeed often times a mistake in this matter, people who are not fit will be puzzling their heads to little purpose, and those who are prove slothful and decline the trouble; and thus it will be if we do not thoroughly understand ourselves, but suffer pride or ease to make the estimate. . . .

We have already expressed our thoughts concerning the capacity and perfection of the understanding, and what has been said if duly considered, is sufficient to bring every particular person acquainted with their own defects. But because they who need amendment most, are commonly least disposed to make such reflections as are necessary to procure it, we will spend a few pages in considering for them, and in observing the most usual defects of the thinking faculty.

If we are of their opinion who say that the understanding is only passive, and that judgment belongs to the will, I see not any defect the former can have, besides narrowness and a disability to extend itself to many things, which is indeed incident to all creatures, the brightest intelligence in the highest order of angels is thus defective, as well as the meanest mortal, though in a less degree. Nor ought it to be complained of, since 'tis natural and necessary, we may as well desire to be gods as desire to know all things. Some sort of ignorance therefore, or nonperception we cannot help; a finite mind, suppose it as large as you please, can never extend itself to infinite truths. But no doubt it is in our power to remedy a great deal more than we do, and probably a larger range is allowed us than the most active and enlightened understanding has hitherto reached. Ignorance then can't be avoided but error may, we cannot judge of things of which we have no idea, but we can suspend our judgment about those of which we have, till clearness and evidence oblige us to pass it. Indeed in strictness of speech the will and not the understanding is blameable when we think amiss, since the latter opposes not the ends for which God made it, but readily extends itself as far as it can, receiving such impressions as are made on it; 'tis the former that directs it to such objects, that fills up its capacity with such ideas as are foreign to its business and of no use to it, or which does not at least oppose the incursions of material things, and deface as much as it is able those impressions which sensible objects leave in the imagination. But since it is not material to the present design, whether judgment belongs to the understanding or will, we shall not nicely distinguish how each of them is employed in acquiring knowledge, but treat of them both together in this chapter, allotted to the service of the studious, who when they are put in the way may by their own meditations and experience, rectify the mistakes and supply the omissions we happen to be guilty of.

They who apply themselves to the contemplation of truth, will perhaps at first find a contraction or emptiness of thought, and that their mind offers nothing on the subject they would consider, is not ready at unfolding, nor in representing correspondent ideas to be compared with it, is as it were asleep or in a dream, and though not empty of all thought, yet thinks nothing clearly or to the purpose. The primary cause of this is that limitation which all created minds are subject to, which limitation appears more visible in some than in others, either because some minds are endowed by their creator with a larger capacity than the rest, or if you are not inclined to think so, then by reason of the indisposition of the bodily organs, which cramps and contracts the operations of the mind. And that person whose capacity of receiving ideas is very little, whose ideas are disordered, and not capable of being so disposed as that they may be compared in order to the forming of a judgment, is a fool or little better. If we find this to be our case, and that after frequent trials there appears no hopes of amendment, 'tis best to desist, we shall but lose our labor, we may do some good in an active life and employments that depend on the body, but we're altogether unfit for contemplation and the exercises of the mind. Yet ere we give out let's see if it be thus with us in all cases; Can we think and argue rationally about a dress, an intrigue, an estate? Why then not upon better subjects? The way of considering and meditating justly is the same on all occasions. 'Tis true, there will fewest ideas arise when we would meditate on such subjects as we've been least conversant about; but this is a fault which it is in our power to remedy, first by reading or discoursing, and then by frequent and serious meditation, of which hereafter.

As those we have been speaking of are hindered in their search after truth, through a want of ideas out of which to deduce it, so there are another sort who are not happy in their enquiries, on account of the multitude and impetuosity of theirs. Volatileness of thought, very pernicious to true science, is a fault which people of warm imaginations and active spirits are apt to fall into. Such a temper is readily disposed to receive errors and very well qualified to propagate them, especially if a volubility of speech be joined to it. These through an immoderate nimbleness of thinking skip from one idea to another, without observing due order and connection, they content themselves with a superficial view, a random glance, and depending on the vigor of their imagination, are took with appearances, never tarrying to penetrate the subject, or to find out truth if she float not upon the surface. A multitude of ideas not relating to the matter they design to think of rush in upon them, and their easy mind entertains all comers how impertinent soever; instead of examining the question in debate they are got into the clouds, numbering the cities in the moon and building airy castles there. Nor is it easy to cure this defect, since it deceives others as well as those who have it with a show of very great ingenuity. The vivacity of such persons makes their conversation plausible, and taking with those who consider not much, though not with the judicious; it procures for them the character of wit, but hinders them from being wise. For truth is not often found by such as won't take time to examine her counterfeits, to distinguish between evidence and probability, realities and appearances, but who through a conceit of their own sharp-sightedness think they can pierce to the bottom with the first glance.

To cure this distemper perfectly perhaps it will be necessary to apply to the body as well as to the mind: The animal spirits must be lessened, or rendered more calm and manageable; at least they must not be unnaturally and violently moved, by such a diet, or such passions, designs and divertisments as are likely to put them in a ferment. Contemplation requires a governable body, a sedate and steady mind, and the body and the mind do so reciprocally influence each other, that we can scarce keep the one in tune if the other be out of it. We can neither observe the errors of our intellect, nor the irregularity of our morals whilst we are darkened by fumes, agitated with unruly passions, or carried away with eager desires after sensible things and vanities. We must therefore withdraw our minds from the world, from adhering to the senses, from the love of material beings, of pomps and gaieties; for 'tis these that usually steal away the heart, that seduce the mind to such unaccountable wanderings, and so fill up its capacity that they leave no room for truth, so distract its attention that it cannot enquire after her. For though the body does partly occasion this fault, yet the will no doubt may in good measure remedy it by using its authority to fix the understanding on such objects as it would have contemplated; it has a rein which will certainly curb this wandering, if it can but be persuaded to make use of it. Indeed attention and deep meditation is not so agreeable to our animal nature, does not flatter our pride so well as this agreeable reverie, which gives us a pretense to knowledge without taking much pains to acquire it, and does not choke us with the humbling thoughts of our own ignorance, with which we must make such ado e're it can be enlightened. Yet without attention and strict examination we are liable to false judgments on every occasion, to vanity and arrogance, to impertinent prating of things we don't understand, are kept from making a progress, because we fancy ourselves to be at the top already, and can never attain to true wisdom. If then we would hereafter think to purpose, we must suffer ourselves to be convinced how oft we have already thought to none, suspect our quickness, and not give our desultory imagination leave to ramble.

And in order to the restraining it we may consider, what a loss of time and study such irregular and useless thoughts occasion, what a reproach they are to our reason, how they cheat us with a *show* of knowledge, which so long as we are under the power of this giddy temper will inevitably escape us. And if to this we add a serious perusal of such books as are not loosely writ, but require an attent and awakened mind to apprehend, and to take in the whole force of them, obliging ourselves to understand them thoroughly, so as to be able to give a just account of them to ourselves, or rather to some other person intelligent enough to take it and to correct our mistakes, it is to be hoped we shall obtain a due poise of mind, and be able to direct our thoughts to the thorough discussion of such subjects as we would examine. Such books I mean as are fuller of matter than words, which diffuse a light through every part of their subject, do not skim, but penetrate it to the bottom, yet so as to leave somewhat to be wrought out by the reader's own meditation; such as are writ with order and connection, the strength of whose arguments can't be sufficiently felt unless we remember and compare the whole system. 'Tis impossible to prescribe absolutely, and every one may easily find what authors are most apt to stay their attention, and should apply to them. But whenever they meditate, be it on what object it may, let them fix their minds steadily on it, not removing till it be thoroughly examined, at least not until they have seen all that's necessary to their present purpose.

Doing so we shall prevent rashness and precipitation in our judgments, which is occasioned by that volatileness we have been speaking of, together with an over-weaning opinion of ourselves. All the irregularities of our will proceed from those false judgments we make, through want of consideration, or a partial examination when we do consider. For did we consider with any manner of attention, we could not be so absurd as to call evil, good, and choose it as such, or prefer a less good before a greater, a poor momentary trifle before the purity and perfection of our mind, before an eternal and immutable crown of glory! But we seek no farther than the first appearances of truth and good, here we stop, allowing neither time nor thought to search to the bottom, and to pull off those disguises which impose on us. This precipitation is that which gives birth to all our errors, which are nothing else but a hasty and injudicious sentence, a mistaking one thing for another, supposing an agreement or disparity amongst ideas and their relations where in reality there is none, occasioned by an imperfect and cursory view of them. And though there are other things which may be said to lead us into error, yet they do it only as they seduce us into rash and precipitate judgments. We love grandeur and every thing that feeds our good opinion of ourselves, and therefore would judge off hand, supposing it a disparagement to our understandings to be long in examining, so that we greedily embrace whatever seems to carry evidence enough for a speedy determination, how slight and superficial soever it be. Whereas did we calmly and deliberately examine our evidence, and how far those motives we are acted by ought to influence, we should not be liable to this seduction. For hereby the impetuosity of a warm imagination would be cooled, and the extravagancies of a disorderly one regulated; we should not be deceived by the report of our senses; the prejudices of education; our own private interest, and readiness to receive the opinions whether true or false of those we love, and would appear to love because we think they will serve us in that interest; our inordinate thirst after a great reputation, or the power and riches, the grandeurs and pleasures of this world, these would no longer dissipate our thoughts and distract our attention, for then we should be sensible how little concern is due to them. We should neither mistake in the end and object by not employing our understandings at all about such things as they were chiefly made for, or not enough, or by busying them with such as are out of their reach, or beneath their application; nor should we be out in the method of our meditation, by going a wrong or a round about way. For the God of truth is ready to lead us into all truth, if we honestly and attentively apply ourselves to him.

In sum, whatever false principle we embrace, whatever

wrong conclusion we draw from true ones, is a disparagement to our thinking power, a weakness of judgment proceeding from a confused and imperfect view of things, as that does from want of attention, and a hasty and partial examination. It were endless to reckon up all the false maxims and reasonings we fall into, nor is it possible to give a list of them, for there are innumerable errors opposite to one single truth. The general causes have been already mentioned, the particulars are as many as those several compositions which arise from the various mixtures of the passions, interests, education, conversation and reading, etc. of particular persons. And the best way that I can think of to improve the understanding, and to guard it against all errors proceed they from what cause they may, is to regulate the will, whose office it is to determine the understanding to such and such ideas, and to stay it in the consideration of them so long as is necessary to the discovery of truth; for if the will be right the understanding can't be guilty of any culpable error. Not to judge of anything which we don't apprehend, to suspend our assent till we see just cause to give it, and to determine nothing till the strength and clearness of the evidence oblige us to it. To withdraw ourselves as much as may be from corporeal things, that pure reason may be heard the better; to make that use of our senses for which they are designed and fitted, the preservation of the body, but not to depend on their testimony in our enquiries after truth. Particularly to divest ourselves of mistaken self-love, little ends and mean designs, and to keep our inclinations and passions under government. Not to engage ourselves so far in any party or opinion as to make it in a manner necessary that that should be right, lest from wishing it were, we come at last to persuade ourselves it is so. But to be passionately in love with truth, as being thoroughly sensible of her excellency and beauty. To embrace her how opposite soever she may sometimes be to our humors and designs, to bring these over to her, and never attempt to make her truckle to them. To be so far from disliking a truth because it touches us home, and lances our tenderest and dearest corruption, as on the contrary to prize it the more, by how much the more plainly it shows us our errors and miscarriages. For indeed it concerns us most to know such truths as these, it is not material to us what other people's opinions are, any farther than as the knowledge of their sentiments may correct our mistakes. And the higher our station is in the world, so much the greater need have we to be curious in this particular.

The mean and inconsiderable often stumble on truth when they seek not after her, but she is commonly kept out of the way, and industriously concealed from the great and mighty; either out of design or envy, for whoever would make a property of another must by all means conceal the truth from him; and they who envy their neighbor's preeminence in other things, are willing themselves to excel in exactness of judgment, which they think and very truly, to be the greatest excellency. And to help forward this deception, the great instead of being industrious in finding out the truth, are generally very impatient when they meet with her. She does not treat them so tenderly and fawningly, with so much ceremony and complaisance as their flatterers do. There is in her that which used to be the character of our nation, and honest plainness and sincerity, openness and blunt familiarity: She cannot mould herself into all shapes to be rendered agreeable, but standing on her native worth is regardless of outside and varnish. But to return from this digression.

Above all things we must be thoroughly convinced of our entire dependence on God, for what we *know* as well as for what we are, and be warmly affected with the sense of it, which will both excite us to practice, and enable us to perform the rest. Though we are naturally dark and ignorant, yet in *his light, we may* hope to *see light,* if with the son of Syrac we petition for *wisdom that sits by his throne* to *labor with us,* and sigh with David after his *light and truth.* For then he who is the light that lightneth everyone who comes into the world, the immutable truth, and uncreated wisdom of his father, will teach us in the way of wisdom and lead us in right paths, he will instruct us infinitely better by the right use of our own faculties than the brightest human reason can. For in him are all the treasures of wisdom and knowledge which he liberally dispenses to all who humbly, honestly and heartily ask them of him. To close this head: Whatever the notion that we see all things in God, may be as to the truth of it, 'tis certainly very commendable for its piety, in that it most effectually humbles the most dangerous sort of pride, the being proud of our knowledge, and yet does not slacken our endeavors after knowledge but rather excites them.

As to the *method* of thinking, if it be proper for me to say anything of that, after those better pens which have treated of it already, it falls in with the subject I'm now come to, which is, that *natural logic* I would propose. I call it natural because I shall not send you further than your own minds to learn it, you may if you please take in the assistance of some well chosen book, but a good natural reason after all, is the best director, without this you will scarce argue well, though you had the choicest books and tutors to instruct you, but with it you may, though you happen to be destitute of the other. For as a very judicious writer on this subject (to whose ingenious remarks and rules I am much obliged) well observes, "These operations (of the mind) proceed merely from nature, and that sometimes more perfectly from those who are altogether ignorant of logic, than from others who have learned it." [Arnauld, *Art of Thinking*]

That which we propose in all our meditations and reasonings is, either to deduce some truth we are in search of, from such principles as we're already acquainted with; or else, to dispose our thoughts and reasonings in such a manner, as to be able to convince others of those truths which we ourselves are convinced of. Other designs indeed men may have, such as the maintenance of their own opinions, actions and parties without regard to the truth and justice of them, or the seduction of their unwary neighbors, but these are mean and base ones, beneath a man, much more a Christian, who is or ought to be endowed with greater integrity and ingenuity.

Now reasoning being nothing else but a comparison of ideas, and a deducing of conclusions from clear and evident principles, it is in the first place requisite that our ideas be clear and just, and our principles true, else all our discourse will be nonsense and absurdity, falsehood and error. And that our idea may be right, we have no more to do but to look attentively into our minds, having as we said above, laid aside all prejudices and whatever may give a false tincture to our light, there we shall find a clear and lively representation of what we seek for, unsophisticated with the dross of false definitions and unintelligible expressions. But we must not imagine that a transient view will serve the turn, or that our eye will be enlightened if it be not fixed. For though truth be exceeding bright, yet since our prejudices and passions have darkened our eye-sight, it requires no little pains and application of mind to find her out, the neglect of which application is the reason that we have so little truth, and that the little we have is almost lost in that rubbish of error which is mingled with it. And since truth is so near at hand, since we are not obliged to tumble over many authors, to hunt after every celebrated genius, but may have it for enquiring after in our own breasts, are we not inexcusable if we do not obtain it? Are we not unworthy of compassion if we suffer our understandings to be overrun with error? Indeed it seems to me most reasonable and most agreeable to the wisdom and equity of the divine operations, that everyone should have a teacher in their own bosoms, who will if they seriously apply themselves to him, immediately enlighten them so far as that is necessary, and direct them to such means as are sufficient for their instruction both in human and divine truths; for as to the latter, reason if it be right and solid, will not pretend to be our sole instructor, but will send us to divine revelation when it may be had.

God does nothing in vain, he gives no power or faculty which he has not allotted to some proportionate use, if therefore he has given to mankind a rational mind, every individual understanding ought to be employed in somewhat worthy of it. The meanest person should think as justly, though not as *capaciously*, as the greatest philosopher. And if the understanding be made for the contemplation of truth, and I know not what else it can be made for, either there are many understandings who are never able to attain what they were designed and fitted for, which is contrary to the supposition that God made nothing in vain, or else the very meanest must be put in a way of attaining it: Now how can this be if all that which goes to the composition of a knowing man in the account of the world, be necessary to make one so? All have not leisure to learn languages and pore on books, nor opportunity to converse with the learned; but all may *think*, may use their own faculties rightly, and consult the master who is within them.

By ideas we sometimes understand in general all that which is the immediate object of the mind, whatever it perceives; and in this large sense it may take in all thought, all that we are any ways capable of discerning: So when we say we have no idea of a thing, 'tis as much as to say we know nothing of the matter. Again, it is more strictly taken for that which represents to the mind some object distinct from it, whether clearly or confusedly; when this is its import, our knowledge is said to be as clear as our ideas are. For that idea which represents a thing so clearly, that by an attent and simple view we may discern its properties and modifications, at least so far as they can be known, is never false; all our certainty and evidence depends on it, if we know not truly what is thus represented to our minds we know nothing. Thus the idea of equality between 2 and 2 is so evident that it is impossible to doubt of it, no arguments could convince us of the contrary, nor be able to persuade us that the same may be found between 2 and 3.

And as such an idea as this is never false, so neither can any idea be said to be so, if by false we mean that which has no existence; our idea certainly exists, though there be not anything in nature correspondent to it. For though there be no such thing as a golden mountain, yet when I think of one, 'tis certain I have an idea of it.

But our ideas are then said to be false, or rather wrong, when they have no conformity to the real nature of the thing whose name they bear. So that properly speaking it is not the idea but the judgment that is false; we err in supposing that our idea is answerable to something without us when it is not. In simple perceptions we are not often deceived, but we frequently mistake in compounding them, by uniting several things which have no agreement, and separating others which are essentially united. Indeed it may happen that our perceptions are faulty sometimes, through the indisposition of the organs or faculties, thus a man who has the *jaundice* sees everything tinged with yellow, yet even here the error is not in the simple idea but in the composed one, for we do not mistake when we say the object appears yellow to our sight, though we do, when we affirm that it does, or ought to do so to others. So again, when the mind does not sufficiently attend to her ideas nor examine them on all sides, 'tis very likely she will think amiss, but this also is a false judgment, that which is amiss in the perception being rather the inadequateness than the falsehood. Thus in many cases we enquire no farther than whether an action be not directly forbidden, and if we do not find it absolutely unlawful, we think that sufficient to authorize the practice of it, not considering it as we ought to do, clothed with the circumstances of scandal, temptation, etc. which place it in the same classes with things unlawful, at least make it so to us.

Rational creatures should endeavor to have right ideas of everything that comes under their cognizance, but yet our ideas of morality, our thoughts about religion are those which we should with greatest speed and diligence rectify, because they are of most importance, the life to come, as well as all the occurences of this, depending on them. We should search for truth in our most abstracted speculations, but it concerns us nearly to follow her close in what relates to the conduct of our lives. For the main thing we are to drive at in all our studies, and that which is the greatest improvement of our understandings is the art of prudence, the being all of a piece, managing all our words and actions as it becomes wise persons and good Christians.

Yet in this we are commonly most faulty; for besides the deceits of our passions, our ideas of particular virtues and vices, goods and evils, being an assemblage of diverse simple perceptions, and including several judgments are therefore liable to mistake, and much more so considering how we commonly come by them. We hear the word that stands for such a thing, suppose honor, and then instead of enquiring what it is at the fountain head the oracles of God, and our own, or the impartial reason of the wisest and the best, custom and the observations we make on the practice of such as pretend to it forms our idea, which is seldom a right one, the opinions and practices of the world being very fallacious, and many times quite opposite to the dictates of reason would we but give ear to them. For what a strange distorted idea of honor must they needs have, who can think it honorable to break a vow that ought to be kept, and dishonorable to get loose from an engagement that ought to be broken? Who cannot endure to be taxed with a lie, and yet never think fit to keep their word? What do they think of greatness who support their pomp at the expense of the groans and tears of many injured families? What is their idea of heaven, who profess to believe such a thing, and yet never endeavor to qualify themselves for the enjoyment of it? Have they any idea at all of these things when they speak of them? Or, if they have, is it not a very false one?

Now that we may avoid mistake the better, and because we usually join words to our ideas even when we only meditate, we should free them from all equivocation, not make use of any word, which has not a distinct idea annexed to it, and where custom has joined many ideas to one word, carefully separate and distinguish them. For if our words are equivocal, how can we by pronouncing such and such, excite the same idea in another that is in our own mind, which is the end of speech, and consequently how can we be understood? And if sometimes we annex one idea to a word, and sometimes another, we may forever wrangle with those who perhaps would be found to agree with us if we understood each other, but can neither convince them, nor clear up the matter to our own mind. For instance: Should I dispute whether evil were to be chosen? Without defining what I mean by evil, which is a word customarily applied to things of different natures, and should conclude in the affirmative, meaning at the same time the evil of pain, or any corporal loss or punishment, I were not mistaken, though another person who annexes no other idea but that of sin to the word evil, might justly contradict me and say that I was. Or if in the process of my discourse, I should without giving notice of it, substitute the idea of sin instead of that of pain, when I mention evil, I should argue falsely. For it is a maxim that we may choose a less evil to avoid a greater, if both of them be corporal evils, or if one of them be so, and we choose it to avoid sin, between which and the evil of pain there is no comparison: But if the two evils proposed to our choice be both of them sinful, that principle will not hold, we must choose neither, whatever comes on it, sin being eligible no manner of way.

Thus many times our ideas are thought to be false when the fault is really in our language, we make use of words without joining any, or only loose and indeterminate ideas to them, prating like parrots who can modify sounds, and pronounce syllables, and sometimes martial them as a man would, though without the use of reason or understanding anything by them. So that after a long discourse and many fine words, our hearer may justly ask us what we have been saying? And what it is we would be at? And so a great part, of the good breeding of the world, many elegant complements pass for nothing, they have no meaning, or if they have, 'tis quite contrary to what the words in other cases signify.

From the comparison of two or more ideas clearly conceived arises a judgment, which we may lay down for a principle, and as we have occasion argue from. Always observing that those judgments which we take for axioms or principles, be such as carry the highest evidence and conviction, such as every one who will but in the least attend may clearly see, and be fully convinced of, and which need not another idea for their demonstration. Thus from the agreement which we plainly perceive between the ideas of God and of goodness singly considered, we discern that they may be joined together so as to form this proposition, that God is good: And from the evident disparity that is between God and injustice, we learn to affirm this other, that he is not unjust. And so long as we judge of nothing but what we see clearly, we can't be mistaken in our judgments, we may indeed in those reasonings and deductions we draw from them, if we are ignorant of the laws of argumentation, or negligent in the observation of them.

The first and principal thing therefore to be observed in all the operations of the mind is, That we determine nothing about those things of which we have not a clear idea, and as distinct as the nature of the subject will permit, for we cannot properly be said to know anything which does not clearly and evidently appear to us. Whatever we see distinctly we likewise see clearly, distinction always including clearness, though this does not necessarily include that, there being many objects clear to the view of the mind, which yet can't be said to be distinct.

That (to use the words of a celebrated author) may be said to be "clear which is present and manifest to an attentive mind; so as we say we see objects clearly, when being present to our eyes they sufficiently act on them, and our eyes are disposed to regard them. And that distinct, which is so clear, particular, and different from all other things, that it contains not anything in itself which appears not manifestly to him who considers it as ought." [Descartes, *Principles of Philosophy*, Pt. 1, 43] Thus we may have a clear, but not a distinct and perfect idea of God and of our own souls; their existence and some of their properties and attributes may be certainly and indubitably known, but we can't know the nature of our souls distinctly, for reasons too long to be mentioned here, and less that of God, because he is infinite. Now where our knowledge is distinct, we may boldly deny of a subject, all that which after a careful examination we find not in it: But where our knowledge is only clear, and not distinct, though we may safely affirm what we see, yet we can't without a hardy presumption deny of it what we see not. And were it not very common to find people both talking and writing of things of which they have no notion, no clear idea; nay and determining dogmatically concerning the entire nature of those of which they cannot possibly have an adequate and distinct one, it might seem impertinent to desire them to speak no farther than they apprehend. They will tell you peremptorily of contradictions and absurdities in such matters as they themselves must allow they cannot comprehend, though others as sharp-sighted as themselves can see no such thing as they complain of.

As judgments are formed by the comparing of ideas, so reasoning or discourse arises from the comparison or combination of several judgments. Nature teaches us when we can't find out what relation one idea bears to another by a simple view or bare comparison, to seek for a common measure or third idea, which relating to the other two, we may by comparing it with each of them, discern wherein they agree or differ. Our invention discovers itself in proposing readily apt ideas for this middle term, our judgment in making choice of such as are clearest and most to our purpose, and the excellency of our reasoning consists in our skill and dexterity in applying them.

Invention indeed is the hardest part, when proofs are found it is not very difficult to manage them. And to know precisely wherein their nature consists, may help us somewhat in our enquiries after them. An intermediate idea then which can make out an agreement between other ideas, must be equivalent to, and yet distinct from those we compare by it. Where ideas agree it will not be hard to find such an equivalent, and if after diligent search we cannot meet with any, 'tis a pretty sure sign that they do not agree. It is not necessary indeed that our middle idea be equivalent in all respects, 'tis enough if it be in such as make the comparison: And when it is so to one of the compared ideas but not to the other, that's a proof that they do not agree amongst themselves.

All the commerce and intercourse of the world is managed by equivalents, conversation as well as traffic. Why do we trust our friends but because their truth and honesty appears to us equivalent to the confidence we repose in them? Why do we perform good offices to others, but because there's a proportion between them and the merit of the person, or our own circumstances? And as the way to know the worth of things is to compare them one with another, so in like manner we come to the knowledge of the truth of them by an equal balancing. But you will say, though I may learn the value of a Spanish coin by weighing, or comparing it with some other money whose standard I know, and so discern what proportion it bears to those goods I would exchange; yet what scales shall I find to weigh ideas? What hand so even as to poise them justly? Or if that might be done, yet where shall I meet with an equivalent idea when I have occasion to use one?

In answer to this demand I consider, that as light is always visible to us if we have an organ to receive it, if we turn our eyes towards it, and that nothing interpose between it and us; so is truth, we are surrounded with it, and God has given us faculties to receive it. If it be asked, why then do we so seldom find it? The reason is, because instead of making right use of our faculties we employ them in keeping it out; we either shut our eyes, or if we vouchsafe to open them, we are sure to view it through such unsuitable mediums as fail not to misrepresent it to us. And for those few noble spirits, who open the windows of their souls to let in truth, and take the films of interest, passion and prejudice from before their eyes, they will certainly be enlightened, and cannot miss of obtaining as much truth as they are capable of receiving. For, to go on with the comparison, as we can see no farther than our own horizon, though the light shine never so bright around us; and as we cannot discern every object even within that compass clearly, nor any distinctly but what we particularly apply ourselves to; so neither are our capacities large enough to take in *all* truth, as has been often said, nor are we capable of attaining *any* without attention and diligent examination. But if we carefully consider those ideas we already have and attend to those truths we are acquainted with, we cannot want mediums to discover more, if our enquiries be after that which is within our reach. He who is the fountain of truth is also a God of order, and has so regularly connected one truth with another, that the discovery of one is a step towards a further progress; so that if we diligently examine those truths which, we know, they will clear the way to what we search after: For it seldom happens but that the question itself directs us to some idea that will serve for the explanation or proof of it.

There is no object, no accident of life but affords us matter of instruction. God has so disposed all the works of his hands, all the actings of his providence, that every one of them ministers to our improvement, if we will but observe and apply them. Indeed this living *ex tempore* which most of us are guilty of, our making no reflections, our gay and volatile humor which transports us in an instant from one thing to another, e're we have with the industrious bee sucked those sweets it would afford us, frequently renders his gracious bounty ineffectual. For as the diligent hand maketh rich, whilst the slothful and prodigal come to nothing, so the use of our powers improves and increases them, and the most observing and considerate is the wisest person: For she lays up in her mind as in a storehouse, ready to produce on all occasions, a clear and simple idea of every object that has at any time presented itself. And perhaps the difference between one woman's reason and another's may consist only in this, that the one has amassed a greater number of such ideas than the other, and disposed them more orderly in her understanding, so that they are at hand, ready to be applied to those complex ideas whose agreement or disagreement cannot be found out but by the means of some of them.

But because examples are more familiar than precepts, as condescending to show us the very manner of practicing them, I shall endeavor to make the matter in hand as plain as I can by subjoining instances to the following rules, which rules as I have not taken wholly on trust from others, so neither do I pretend to be the inventer of them.

We have heard already that a medium is necessary when we can't discern the relation that is between two or more ideas by intuition or a simple view. Could this alone procure us what we seek after, the addition of other ideas would be needless, since to make a show of wit by tedious arguings and unnecessary flourishes, does only perplex and encumber the matter, intuition being the simplest, and on that account the best way of knowing.

Rule I. And therefore we should in the first place, acquaint ourselves thoroughly with the state of the question, have a distinct notion of our subject whatever it be, and of the terms we make use of, knowing precisely what it is we drive at: that so we may in the second

Rule II. Cut off all needless ideas and whatever has not a connection to the matter under consideration, which serve only to fill up the capacity of the mind, and to divide and distract the attention. From the neglect of this comes those causeless digressions, tedious parentheses and impertinent remarks which we meet with in some authors. For, as when our sight is diffused and extended to many objects at once we see none of them distinctly; so when the mind grasps at every idea that presents itself, or rambles after such as relate not to its present business, it loses its hold and retains a very feeble apprehension of that which it should attend. Some have added another rule (viz.) that we reason only on those things of which we have clear ideas; but I take it to be a consequence of the first, and therefore do not make it a distinct one: For we can by no means understand our subject, or be well acquainted with the state of the question, unless we have a clear idea of all its terms.

Rule III. Our business being stated, the next rule is to conduct our thoughts by order, beginning with the most simple and easy objects, and ascending as by degrees to the knowledge of the more composed. I need not tell you, that order makes everything, easy, strong and beautiful, and that the superstructure is neither like to last or please unless the foundation be duly laid, for this is obvious to the most superficial reader. Nor are they likely to solve the difficult, who have neglected or slightly passed over the easy questions. Our knowledge is gradual, and by passing regularly through plain things, we arrive in due time at the more abstruse.

Rule IV. In this method we are to practice the fourth rule which is, not to leave any part of our subject unexamined, it being as necessary to consider all that can let in light, as to shut out what's foreign to it. We may stop short of truth as well as overrun it; and though we look never so attentively on our proper object, if we view but half of it, we may be as much mistaken, as if we extended our sight beyond it. Some objects agree very well when observed on one side, which upon turning the other show a great disparity. Thus the right angle of a triangle may be like to one part of a square, but compare the whole, and you'll find them very different figures. And a moral action may in some circumstance be not only fit but necessary, which in others, where time, place, and the like have made an alteration, would be most improper; so that if we venture to act on the former judgment, we may easily do amiss, if we would act as we ought, we must view its new face, and see with what aspect that looks on us.

To this rule belongs that of dividing the subject of our meditations into as many parts, as we can, and as shall be requisite to understand it perfectly. This is indeed most necessary in difficult questions, which will scarce be unravelled but in this manner by pieces: Ever taking care to make exact reviews, and to sum up our evidence justly e're we pass sentence and fix our judgment.

Rule V. To which purpose we must always keep our subject directly in our eye, and closely pursue it through all our progress; there being no better sign of a good understanding than thinking closely and pertinently, and reasoning dependently, so as to make the former part of our discourse a support to the latter, and *this* an illustration of *that*, carrying light and evidence in every step we take. The neglect of this rule is the cause why our discoveries of truth are seldom exact, that so much is often said to so little purpose; and many intelligent and industrious readers when they have read over a book are very little wiser than when they began it. And that the two last rules may be the better observed, 'twill be fit very often to look over our process so far as we have gone, that so by rendering our subject familiar, we may the sooner arrive to an exact knowledge of it.

Rule VI. All which being done we are in a fair way towards keeping the last rule, which is, to judge no further than we perceive, and not to take anything for truth which we do not evidently know to be so. Indeed in some cases we are forced to content ourselves with probability, but 'twere well if we did so only where 'tis plainly necessary. That is, when the subject of our meditation is such as we cannot possibly have a certain knowledge of, because we are not furnished with proofs which have a constant and immutable connection with the ideas we apply them to, or because we cannot perceive it, which is our case in such exigencies as oblige us to act presently, on a cursory view of the arguments proposed to us, when we want time to trace them to the bottom, and to make use of such means as would discover truth.

Catharine Trotter Cockburn

CATHARINE TROTTER was born on August 16, 1679. Her father was a sea captain and was reported to be a favorite of Charles II, but when Trotter was quite young, he went down with his ship, carrying the family fortunes with him. She seems to have been able to procure for herself a remarkably extensive education, learning French, Latin, Greek, and even logic. She also seems to have undertaken to provide some of her family's financial support at a young age, writing five plays, the first of which appeared when she was only seventeen. She took as well an interest in the philosophical issues of her day, particularly as they touched on religious matters, at the age of twenty publishing a defense of Locke. Her early letters, especially those to her friend George Burnet of Kemnay, who for a time lived at the court in Hanover that housed Leibniz, show her engaged in the intellectual controversies of her day. In one, she gives a spirited defense of Lady Masham, whose letters to Leibniz Burnet had seen. Burnet had apparently suggested Masham was not the author of the ideas in these letters, and Trotter chides: "I pray be more equitable to her sex, than the generality of yours are: who, when any thing is written by a woman, that they cannot deny their approbation to, are sure to rob us of the glory of it, by concluding 'tis not her own; or at least, that she had some assistance, which has been said in many instances to my knowledge unjustly"

(*Works*, II, 190). In 1708, she married a clergyman named Cockburn, and, we are told, was diverted from her studies by the duties of raising a large family in reduced circumstances. In later years, however, she returned to her intellectual pursuits, and we find her engaging in a correspondence with a niece, in which she served as mentor, and eventually reentering the arena of philosophical controversy. She died on May 11, 1749, at the age of 71, and the task of editing her collected works, on which she had begun, was completed by a family friend, Thomas Birch. After her death, Birch published a two-volume collection of her philosophical works, to which he added one of her plays, some poems, and a collection of her letters, prefaced by an account that he wrote of her life. At the end of this biography, Birch reminds us of the circumstances in which Catharine Trotter Cockburn did her work: "But her abilities as a writer, and the merit of her works, will not have full justice done them, without a due attention to the peculiar circumstances, in which they were produced, her early youth, when she wrote some; her very advanced age, and ill state of health, when she drew up others; the uneasy situation of her fortune, during the whole course of her life; and an interval of near twenty years, in the vigor of it, spent in the cares of a family, without the least leisure for reading or contemplation: After which, with a mind so long diverted and encumbered, resuming her studies, she instantly recovered its entire powers, and in the hours of relaxation from her domestic employments pursued, to their utmost limits, some of the deepest inquiries, of which the human mind is capable" (*Works*, I, xlviii).

Catharine Trotter Cockburn's works, as Birch suggests, fall into several batches. Before her marriage she wrote and published her plays and a defense of Locke's *Essay* against an anonymous attack, actually written by Thomas Burnet, a student of Cudworth's. Much later, in 1726 she published a response to a sermon by a Dr. Holdsworth, attacking Locke for having controverted the doctrine of the resurrection. She subsequently wrote, but failed to get published, a much longer vindication of Locke against Holdsworth, in which she returns to and develops fully one of the themes addressed in the replies to Burnet: The implications of Locke's distinctions of person, man, and substance for the doctrine of the resurrection. Her final works were published in 1743 and 1747. They are again directed against the works of others, and primarily address another of the issues originally discussed in the defense against Burnet, the nature of moral obligation.

The *Vindication of an Essay concerning Human Understanding,* from which this selection was taken, was written in order to show that Locke's *Essay* establishes morality on a firm foundation, a task that she sees as of invaluable service to religion. In it, she addresses three main issues. She argues first, that Locke has an adequate epistemological foundation for morality, grounding it on what suits our nature, which is, in turn, what is required of us by our Maker. Second, she shows that none of Locke's remarks about the soul should lead us to suppose the soul is not immortal, and finally, she discusses the notion of a "natural conscience," arguing that this amounts to nothing more than a human ability to judge our actions right or wrong according to some rule. The vindication of Locke was published anonymously, lest the author's sex lead people to take it less seriously, as she explains in a letter to George Burnet. Locke, however, was able to track down the name of its author, sending Trotter a letter of thanks, together with a present of some books and a sum of money.

✧ Selections from
A Defense of Mr. Locke's Essay of Human Understanding

That the immortality of the soul is only highly probable by the light of nature, none can deny, who believes that apostle, by

---

Selections from Catharine Trotter Cockburn, *A Defense of Mr. Locke's Essay of Human Understanding.* In Thomas Birch, *The Works of Mrs. Catharine Cockburn* (London: J. and P. Knapton, 1751), 69-92.

whom we are told, that life and immortality is brought to light by Jesus Christ through the gospel. Why then is it objected against Mr. Locke's principles, that they give us no certainty of the immortality of the soul without revelation? By what other way can we be certain of anything, that is only highly probable by the light of nature? Which is all that can be proved by any principles; and so far Mr. Locke's will go, as I doubt not to make appear. But farther I shall show that there is nothing in his principles, which at all weakens the main proofs of a future state; so that if they are thought to amount to demonstration, they have no less force and evidence, upon his principles, which will leave no pretense on this account against them; as will plainly appear in examining the Remarker's objections.

You suppose (says he) that the soul may be sometimes absolutely without thoughts, of one kind or other; and also, that God may, if he pleases (for anything we know by the light of nature) give, or have given, to some systems of matter a power to conceive and think. Upon these two suppositions, I could not make out any certain proof of the immortality of the soul, and am apt to think it cannot be done.

As to the first of these objections, I confess I do not see of what consequence it is at all to the proofs of the immortality of the soul: Do they depend upon the contrary supposition, that the soul *always thinks?* If they do, proofs upon a supposition have a very unsure foundation. But let it be granted, that it is ever so clearly proved, that thinking is necessary to the soul's existence, that can no more prove, that it shall always exist, than it proves, that it has always existed; it being as possible for that omnipotence, which from nothing gave the soul a *being*, to deprive it of that *being* in the midst of its most vigorous reflections, as in an utter suspension of all thought. If then this proposition, that the soul always thinks, does not prove, that it is immortal, the contrary supposition takes not away any proof of it; for it is no less easy to conceive, that a *being*, which has the power of thinking with some intervals of cessation from thought, that has existed here for some time in a capacity of happiness or misery, may be continued in, or restored to the same state, in a future life, than that a *being*, which always thinks, may be continued in the same state. But to do the Remarker all the justice, and give him all the satisfaction I can, I shall examine the substance of what he objected against Mr. Locke's assertion, without entering farther into the dispute, than may serve to show, whether it is of any consequence for, or against, the immortality of the soul.

Mr. Locke says, men do not think in sound sleep; and his reason is, because they are not *conscious* of it, and it is a contradiction to say a man thinks, but is not conscious of it; thinking consisting in that very thing of our being *conscious* of it. Upon which supposition, the Remarker *cannot make out any certain proof of the immortality of the soul.*

I suppose Mr. Locke did not design it a proof of the immortality of the soul: but let us see, whether it weakens any proof of it, which the Remarker should have shown, but instead of that proposes difficulties, which that supposition involves him in, and begins with this notable one, I wonder how you can observe, that your soul sometimes does not think; for when you do observe it, you think: if a man could think, and not think, at the same time, he might be able to make this observation. This reversed may be an argument of some force indeed; but to conclude, that my soul does not always think, 'tis sufficient to know, that there has some time past, in which I was not conscious, that I thought; unless we will allow, that the *soul* may think, when the *man* does not, which is plainly to make them two *persons,* as Mr. Locke has shown p. 44, and 45, in which the Remarker says he does not understand what that discourse about the identity or nonidentity of the same man, sleeping and waking, and about Castor and Pollux, aims at, and tends to. A discourse about the *nonidentity of the same man* would, I confess, be very hard to understand; but I find no such in that place, or any other of Mr. Locke's *Essay*: he does not trifle at that rate, as to talk of the *same man's* not being the *same man.* He says indeed, that if the soul can, whilst the body is sleeping, have its thinking and enjoyments apart, which the man is not at all conscious of; his soul, when he sleeps, and the man consisting of body and soul; when he is waking, are two persons. And he further illustrates the same thing in his discourse of Castor and Pollux, which, if it be thought absurd to assert, 'tis not hard to find what that discourse aimed at, *v.g.* to show, that such an absurdity will follow from this supposition, that the soul thinks, when the man is not conscious of it. But whatever that discourse aims at, of what consequence can it be to the immortality of the soul, supposing it *does not* always think? That the Remarker says nothing of. But it will not be improper here to take notice of an inference he draws from it in his second remarks; that Mr. Locke does not think the soul a *permanent substance* distinct from the body. This (says he) seems to be the supposition you go upon, when you question, whether a man waking and sleeping without thoughts be the same man. If there be still the same soul, the same permanent substance, I see no room for that question, or doubt, which you make. Here the question is again turned, not only from the same *person* to the same *man*, but to sleeping *without* thoughts, from sleeping *with* thoughts, that he is *not conscious of;* which are very different cases as to this question, though much the same indeed, as to the thing itself; but that the Remarker won't allow. But perhaps he takes the *soul, man,* and *person,* to signify the same thing, and so they may to him: every man has the liberty to make his own words stand for what idea he pleases; but when he argues against the opinion of another, he must consider in what sense those terms are used by that other, and in that sense oppose him; otherwise he fights with his own notions, and not his, whom he seems to dispute with. And 'tis impossible to read Mr. Locke's *Essay* with the least attention, and not know, that he does not use those three terms in one and the same signification; which if the Remarker had considered, he could not have so much mistaken Mr. Locke, or found such difficulties in his discourse. If Mr. Locke had understood by the *soul, man,* and *person,* the same thing, he would never have made such a question, whether the *soul* thinking apart, what the *man* is not at all conscious of, were not a *distinct person,* from the *man;* which would be just the same thing, as to ask, whether the soul thinking apart, what the soul is not conscious of, be not a distinct soul from the soul: But understanding by *person,* as he does, *self consciousness,* and by *man* the *soul and body united,* he may question, whether the *same soul,* the *same permanent substance,* thinking *apart from the body* in sound sleep, what the waking *man* is not conscious of, whether that *incommunicable consciousness* does not make the *soul,* and the *man* consisting of body and soul, two distinct persons; *personal identity*, according to him, consisting in the *same consciousness*, and not in the same *substance:* for whatever substance there is, without *consciousness* there is no *person. Consciousness* therefore, and not *substance*, making a *person*, the same consciousness must make the same person, whether in the same, or in different substances; and no farther than the same consciousness extends, can there be the same person: but wherever there are *two distinct incommunicable consciousnesses*, there are two distinct *persons*, though in the same substance.

But farther, not only Mr. Locke's question may be made, supposing the soul a *distinct permanent substance*, but he could not make it upon any other supposition with the least sense, to his purpose, which is to confute this opinion, that the *soul* thinks, in sound sleep, when the *man* is not conscious of it. Now what manner of argument, I pray, would this make?

If the soul thinks, when the man is not conscious of it, the *soul* and the *man* are two *persons*.

But the soul not being permanent substance, *may* make two persons. Ergo, the soul *cannot* think, when the man does not, because that makes them two persons; the sum of which is, the soul *cannot* think apart, because it *can*.

But if this assertion, that the soul and the man are two persons, implies, that it is not a permanent substance, let those look to it, who say, that the *soul* thinks, when the *man* is not conscious of it, since it is only a consequence of that supposition; but can no way concern Mr. Locke, who denies that supposition. But the Remarker is to be excused for making an inference so inconsistent with the design of that discourse, since he confesses he does not understand what it tends to, and perhaps only ventured at a shrewd guess to provoke a clearer account. And indeed, the best construction I can make of the Remarker's writing against Mr. Locke's *Essay,* is, that he understands very little of it; so groundless are the difficulties he makes, and his consequences so wrong. This I am sure, no man that means well, if he understands anything of what Mr. Locke says upon this subject, that men think not always, can from thence infer, that he does not think the soul a permanent substance; for it is plain, all the difficulties he finds in supposing the soul does always think, arise only from its being in a sleeping, and waking man, the same permanent substance. Why else does he find it so very hard to be conceived, that the soul in a sleeping man should this moment be busy a thinking; and the next moment in a waking man, not remember, nor be able to recollect one jot of all those thoughts? Why, does he think it strange, if the soul has ideas of its own, that it derived not from sensation or reflection, that it should never, in its private thinking, retain any of them, the very moment it wakes out of them; and then make the man glad with new discoveries? Or why does he call it an absurdity, to make the soul and the man two persons? There is nothing strange or absurd in all this, if the soul in a sleeping and *waking* man be not the same permanent substance.

I hope what has been said, is sufficient to help the Remarker's understanding in that discourse of Mr. Locke's, which so much puzzled him; and then I am certain he cannot apprehend it of any consequence to the immortality of the soul, supposing *it does not think, when the man is not conscious of it.* I now proceed to his second difficulty.

I do not understand (says he) how the soul, if she be at any time utterly without thoughts, what it is, that produces the first thought again, at the end of that unthinking interval. And what then? Must we therefore conclude it cannot be done? If that be a good argument, we must deny the most common and visible operations in nature. Do you understand *how* your soul thinks at all? *How* it passes from one thought to another? *How* it preserves its treasure of ideas, to produce them at pleasure on occasions? And recollects those it had not in a long time reflected on? *How* it moves your body, or is affected by it? These are operations, which I suppose you are not so skeptical as to doubt of; nor yet pretend to understand how they are done: and since we are certain, that the soul is affected with all the considerable changes of the body, that it is sick, and in pain, and unable to perform its functions, according as the body is disordered; since we so sensibly perceive it to become drowsy, when the body is so; so many degrees abated of its action, even to very near not thinking at all, from that intenseness and vigor of thought it had, and recovers, when the body is refreshed with sleep; whatever is the cause of these effects, whether some immediate connection between them, or an arbitrary law of their union; where is the difficulty to conceive, that the same cause, which lulls it almost, should lay it quite to rest, and awaken it again with the body?

But upon this supposition (says the Remarker) that all our thoughts perish in sound sleep, we seem to have a new soul every morning. That is a pretty conceit indeed, but how does this seem? Thus, as he explains himself; if a body cease to move, and come to perfect rest, the motion it had cannot be restored, but a new motion may be produced. If all cogitation be extinct, all our ideas are extinct, so far as they are cogitations, and seated in the soul: so we must have them new impressed, we are, as it were, new born, and begin the world again. The force of which argument lies thus: *cogitation* in the soul answering to *motion* in the body; as the same motion cannot be restored, but a new *motion* may be produced; so the same *cogitations* cannot be restored, but new *cogitations* must be produced. Ergo, we seem to have a new *soul* every morning. This may be a good consequence, when the Remarker has proved, that every *new motion* makes, or seems to make a *new body*. In the meantime, all I can infer from this parallel, is, that my thoughts today are not the same numerical thoughts I had yesterday; which, I believe, nobody supposes they are, though they did not suspect they had a *new soul* with every *new thought*.

But if the Remarker thinks, that if all our thoughts cease in sound sleep, all our ideas are extinct, and must be new impressed; I desire him to consider, when a sleeping or waking man thinks, what becomes of all those ideas, which he does not actually perceive in his own mind; for the mind is capable of taking notice but of very few at once: must not all the rest by this argument be extinct? And so we must have them new impressed; and are, as it were, new born, whenever we have any ideas, which we have not always actually perceived, i.e. every time we pass from one thought to another. This is a sure consequence, if, when all our thoughts cease, all our ideas must be new impressed, unless a man could actually perceive all the ideas he ever had at once; for his having only one thought in his mind can no more keep any other there, or excite any other; that it has no connection with than if he had no thought at all. I am thinking, for example, in my sleep, of a horse; his beauty, strength, and usefulness: does this thought preserve in my mind the idea of a church, of happiness or misery? Or can it help me to any of them, when I have occasion for them? If not, then these ideas must be new impressed, when I awake; but if they remain in the soul, when I was only thinking of a horse, wherever they are bestowed, it may be presumed, there is room for that one idea more without thrusting out another to give it place; and when that one is among them, I see no more reason, why they must be all new impressed, than that the other must have been new impressed, when I only thought of that one; unless it be supposed, that the soul has always just one idea more than there is place for in the repository of its ideas; and if that happen to crowd in, before another has got out, they will all be stifled together, or fly away for air.

But here the Remarker interposes, If you say the ideas remain in the soul, and need only a new excitation; why then, say I, may not infants have innate ideas (which you so much oppose) that want only objects and occasions to excite and actuate them, with a fit disposition of the brain? By what hath been said, it will appear, that this argument gains no force from Mr. Locke's opinion, that the soul does not always think; since if the soul does always think, it can perceive but very few ideas at once; so that the same consequence will follow from a man's having only one thought, as from his having no thought at all; whether all his other ideas must be new impressed, or remain in the soul, and need only a new excitation. This objection therefore would have been as much to the purpose in any other place the Remarker might have asked, if when a man thinks only upon one object, there remain ideas in the soul, which he does not perceive to be there; why may not infants have *innate ideas*, that want only occasions to excite them? This then, having no particular relation to the question in dispute, requires no answer here: but that the Remarker may not think he has entangled Mr. Locke with his own principles, I desire him to consider, if these are parallel cases, how comes it, that when objects or occasions excite these ideas in children, they do not perceive, that they were in their minds before; but consider them as things new, and till then absolutely unknown to them? But when ideas are excited in a man, which he has before received by sensation or reflection, he considers them as things he is acquainted with, and clearly perceives they have been in his mind before. Why does not everything appear equally new to a man, which he has, or has not known before, as every idea does, the first time it is excited in him? But since it is certain, that the mind does perceive when any ideas are excited in it, that were there before; and that every idea appears new to it the first time it is excited; this can be no argument, that because the soul is capable of retaining the ideas it has received by sensation or reflection; that it can record them for its use, and recollect them at pleasure; therefore, it may have innate ideas, though it never perceives, that it had them, not even when they are excited in it; for this makes the cases so far from being the same, that it is one of the greatest arguments against *innate ideas*, that the mind does always perceive, when the ideas, which are excited in it, were there before. Besides, how can it be conceived, that *innate ideas* should need any objects to excite them; and that the mind should never excite any of them in itself without those objects; as it often does excite in itself the ideas it received by sensation, or reflection, without the presence of those objects, by which it first received them. Why then are such objects necessary to excite *innate ideas*, since the mind has a power of exciting ideas in itself, without the presence of any object? When the remarker has shown the reason of this considerable difference, and proved, that it does not hinder them from being parallel cases; then we may conclude against Mr. Locke, that since the soul can retain the ideas it has received, and excite them at pleasure, though it do not always perceive them, therefore it may have ideas, which it never did perceive, nor can excite in itself, nor, when they are excited, perceive, that it ever had them before; and then he can have nothing to say for himself, but must let us enjoy our *unperceivable ideas*, and be as much the better, and wiser for them, as we can.

But still the soul may be sometimes without any thought, and yet (for anything we have heard) not endanger its immortality. Let us consider the Remarker's next difficulty.

Besides (says he) I am utterly at a loss, how to frame any idea of a dead soul, or of a spirit without life or thoughts. How a dead soul comes in here, I do not know. Can there be no life, where there is no thought? I confess, that I have hitherto thought, that insects and plants have life, though I did not suppose, that they do always think. He goes on: What is the soul, when she does not think? She must be actually something, if she exist. She must then have some properties, whereby she is distinguished from nothing, and from matter. And again, in the second remark, you say the soul has no extension, nor at certain fits any cogitation. What can the soul be then but a certain power acting in the body, when the body is prepared for the exercise of it; and ceasing to act, when the body is indisposed? To which I answer, that it is true, we have no idea of the soul but by her operations; but that is no more a reason to conclude, that she is nothing when she does not operate, than when she does, since we are equally ignorant what the soul is, when we do think, as when we do not. I ask what is the soul when she does think? Is she a real permanent substance? What then are her peculiar properties, whereby she is distinguished from other substances? If it be said the power of thinking; I ask, whether she has any other properties to distinguish her from nothing, and from matter? If not, then nothing, or matter, may have the power of thinking. This is plain, if the soul has no essential properties distinct from matter, whereby she alone is capable of the power of thinking, there can be no reason, why matter may not have that power. If it be said she has other essential properties, without which she could not have the power of thinking, when the Remarker has found out what those properties are, he will then know what the soul is, when she does not think; for whatever that substance is, that has the power of thinking, there is no reason to doubt, that it remains the same, when it ceases from that action, any more than there is to doubt, that a body in motion, and at rest, is the same substance; for we have no clearer idea of the substance of body, than we have of the substance of spirit, as Mr. Locke has shown; which excellent discourse alone one would have thought sufficient to prevent the least insinuation, that he does not think the soul a real permanent substance.

There is much more reason to conclude, that those do not think the soul a real permanent substance, who make this question, If the soul has no extension, nor at certain fits any cogitation, what can the soul be then, but a certain power acting in the body, when the body is prepared, etc. For from what other reason can they make it? If the soul be really something else than a certain power acting in the body, what can hinder it from being the same thing, when it does not act? But if it must be nothing, when it is not in action, what then can the soul be, but a certain power acting in the body, when the body is prepared for the exercise of it, and ceasing to be when the body is indisposed? But (to retort the Remarker's words) whether that be a superior divine power distinct from matter, as a *vis movens*, or a power fastened, I know not how, to the body, or upon such and such systems of matter; whether I say of these two suppositions better agrees with this doctrine, I cannot certainly tell; but either of them destroys the immortality of the soul, upon the dissolution of the body. I leave the reader to judge, which is most concerned in this consequence, Mr. Locke, who says, that it is not necessary to the existence of the soul, that it should be always in action; which would be absurd to say, if it be not a *distinct permanent substance;* or the Remarker, who thinks the soul cannot exist, when it is not in action; which there is no ground to think, if it be a *real permanent substance.*

The vanity of men seems to be the great reason, why they have so readily supposed, without any proof, that the soul does always think; for having no idea of it, but by its operations, we are unwilling to perceive our own ignorance, and loath to part with the only idea we have of that dear thing which we call self. On this account the Remarker seems offended with Mr. Locke. Why (says he) do you affirm or introduce a new and unintelligible state of the soul, whereof neither you, nor others, can have any conception? And why is this complained of, but that men are willing to believe they know more than they do? Or how else could they think a state of *thinking, without being conscious of it,* more intelligible, than a state of not thinking at all? Or how could they conclude thinking, which is the action of the soul, necessary to the existence of the soul itself, if they did not make our knowledge the measure of things, and our not having an idea of a thing, sufficient to exclude it from being? I proceed

Then after all (says he) what security can we have upon this supposition that we shall not fall into this sleep at death, and so continue without life or thought? What I have said in the beginning of my discourse upon this head, might serve for an answer to this objection; but the remarker, by repeating it, page 12, seeming to lay a great weight on it, I shall consider it more particularly.

And first (as I observed before) if our security of a future state depends upon this, *that the soul always thinks,* it has a very unsure foundation; for there is no pretense of a proof, that the soul does always think; and there are great probabilities, that it does not think in sound sleep (as Mr. Locke has shown). But if the proofs of a future state do not depend upon the soul's always thinking, the contrary supposition cannot lessen our security of it; and that they do not depend upon it, I think needs not be proved, nobody, that I know of, did ever offer this proposition, *that the soul does always think,* as a proof of its immortality. And the reasons we have to expect a future state are of such a nature, that they can receive no force from it, nor lose any by the contrary supposition. The Remarker on another occasion tells Mr. Locke, the grounds of our expectation of future punishments and rewards are, that there is a presage of them from natural conscience; and that they are deducible from the nature of God, if we allow him moral attributes. Now it is evident, that neither of these two grounds can lose any of their force upon this supposition, that the soul does not think in sound sleep, and will not they secure us, that we shall not continue in this sleep after death? If not, why does the Remarker mention them as proofs of a future state? But if they do prove it, why does he say, he could make out no certain proof of the immortality of the soul, upon this supposition, that it is sometimes without thoughts? Since those proofs he mentions remain in their full force, notwithstanding this supposition. Thus having shown, that all the consequences the Remarker draws from Mr. Locke's supposition are without grounds, I may with assurance conclude, that it is of no consequence to the immortality of the soul, nor does at all weaken any proof of it.

I cannot here forbear taking notice, how little service they do to religion, who establish the main principles of it upon such an uncertain foundation, as the nature of a thing, of which we are so very ignorant, as we certainly are, of *what the soul is*. Her operations we have clear ideas of; and therefore from our capacity of discerning and choosing good or evil; and from the power, wisdom, and goodness of God, which we may certainly know to belong to his nature; we have very good arguments, and great probabilities of a future state of punishments and rewards; such as no considering man can deny, and within everyone's understanding. But when the soul's immortality is said to depend upon such suppositions as this, *that the soul always thinks*, or that it is *immaterial;* what can the consequence be, but to make men think they have very little assurance of a future life, when they find themselves so much in the dark as to those principles, upon which it is established, that the greatest proofs of them are drawn from our ignorance? As that we cannot *conceive how* matter should be capable of such and such powers as we perceive in the soul; or (as the Remarker objects) *what* the soul is, when she is without thoughts.

But could the immateriality of the soul be proved to be as certain, as it is highly probable, it can never be of good consequence, and may be dangerous, to make that the main proof of its immortality; for this is an argument of no use to the generality of mankind, who want either leisure, or capacity, for such nice speculations; and if they are convinced on other grounds, that the soul is immortal, it is no great matter, whether they think it immaterial, or no. But if they are persuaded, that it cannot be immortal, if it is not immaterial, 'tis easy to see of how ill consequence that must be, if the proofs of the soul's immateriality should not happen to convince them; as it often falls out by the different cast of men's heads, that the same arguments, that are very strong and persuasive to one man, have no force at all with another, especially in abstract reflections. Those, therefore, who are zealous for truth, should endeavor to establish it upon the plainest, and clearest principles, and such as are most adapted to common apprehensions. This is not the only instance, in which I have observed, that truth does not suffer less from those who would maintain it upon false or uncertain grounds, than from those, who openly oppose it. I have known several, who have been carefully enough instructed in their duty, who yet for want of being taught at first, or applying themselves to consider the true grounds of it, have been easily argued out of their good notions, though some of them persons of no mean capacity; for if the foundation fail, the best super-structure will fall, though strong and immoveable, when estab-lished upon its proper grounds. And this does not only happen, when the foundation is in itself weak or uncertain, but when truths are taught upon principles, which, though true, and solid in themselves, are not the ground or reason of those truths; which some have done out of a good design of rendering the truths they teach the more sacred. But everything stands firmest on its own foundation: and I believe, if it were rightly consid-ered, it would appear, that the reasons of all moral truths are plain and clear, and within the reach of the lowest apprehen-sions. These things, which I have only hinted at, are of great consequence to be thoroughly considered by all, who have the instruction of others under their care, that they may not think they sufficiently acquit themselves of their duty by inculcating good maxims, when their negligence, or *mistaken zeal* in teach-ing the grounds of them, may at least give too great advantage to those, who make it their business to corrupt the *principles,* as well as the *practice* of their companions, which are but too many in this libertine age.

This being a matter of so universal concern, I hope I shall be excused, if I have led the reader a little out of the way for it. We now return to the Remarker, who, after he has repeated his last difficulty, i.e. If the soul be sometimes without thoughts, why may she not be so, thoughtless, and senseless, after death? he adds, it is some comfort, indeed, that we shall at length return to life at the resurrection: but I know not how you explain that; nor how far you allow us to be the same men, and the same per-sons then that we are now. This is a great comfort indeed, and I suppose the Remarker here designed to make Mr. Locke amends for all the faults he has imputed to his principles, by owning, that they afford us this comfort; but I cannot guess what *that* is which he knows not *how* Mr. Locke explains. Mr. Locke never attempted, that I know of, to explain *how* we shall return to life, which *that* seems to refer to, nor how far we shall then be the same *men;* and he needed not have told him, that he knows not how he explains a thing, which he has not explained at all. But Mr. Locke has very clearly explained how far he allows us to be the same *persons,* consciousness according to him, as far as it is extended, makes the same person, in which, he says, is founded all the right, and justice, of reward, and punishment, happiness, and misery. And thus, he says, we may without any difficulty conceive at the resurrection, the same person, though in a body not exactly in make or parts the same he had here, the same consciousness going along with the soul that inhabits it: Which may be sufficient to satisfy the Remarker how St. Peter at the resurrection will be the same; and how Mr. Locke conceives the resurrection, as far as is revealed of it, and to all its ends and purposes, which is our *happiness,* or *misery.* Further than this he does not pretend, nor are we concerned to know; and I think, in a matter which can only be known by revelation, no man ought to determine, or enquire farther than the Holy Spirit has thought fit to reveal. Mr. Locke knows too well the vanity and presumption of such an attempt, to offer at it. "It is enough (says he) that every one shall appear before the judgment seat of Christ, to receive according to what he had done in his former life; but in what sort of body he shall appear, or of what particles made up, the scripture having said nothing, but that it shall be a spiritual body raised in incorruption, it is not for me to determine." The Remarker must be contented *to walk in the dark* as to these things, though he says he does not love it, since there is no way to have farther light in them than the Scripture has given. And if he thinks Mr. Locke's doctrine of the soul obscure, because he does not pretend to be certain by his natural faculties of things, which they cannot certainly discover (a way to knowledge, which some are very fond of) I believe Mr. Locke will be content not to be understood by him, rather than write what he does not understand himself, to appear intelligible to others.

The Remarker next proceeds to the second supposition, which he thinks weakens the proofs of the immortality of the soul, viz. That God may give, or have given, for any thing we know, to some systems of matter, a power to perceive, and think.

And here one would expect he should have shown how this supposition weakens the proofs of the soul's immortality; but all his objections are against the probability of the supposition, and to show the difficulties of conceiving how matter should have such a power; which he enlarges upon in his third remark, and has several pages to that purpose, for what reason I know not, since Mr. Locke allows it to be highly probable, that the soul is immaterial, but where he is speaking of demonstration, only says, that it is not *impossible, for anything we know,* that God may give, or have given, to some systems of matter, disposed as he sees fit, a power to perceive and think. But my design being only to vindicate Mr. Locke's principles from the dangerous consequences imputed to them by the Remarker, I shall not enter into that dispute; and I think Mr. Locke has said enough, in his last additions, to silence the triumph of such sort of arguments, drawn from *the unconceiveableness of something in one hypothesis,* which cannot be a proof of the contrary opinion, in which there are things altogether as inexplicable, and as far remote from our comprehension. All the demonstration we can have from such difficulties, is of the weakness and scantiness of our knowledge, which should not make us forward in determining positively on either side, much less to establish the immortality of the soul on so uncertain a foundation; which is a consideration I have before insisted on, and I cannot but think Mr. Locke has done much more service to religion in that discourse, *B.* iii. *c.* 4, where, after he had said, that he "sees no contradiction in it, that omnipotency should give to certain systems of matter a power to perceive and think, though it be most highly probable, that the soul is immaterial"; he adds that "if our faculties cannot arrive to demonstrative certainty about it, we need not think it strange: all the great ends of morality and religion are well enough secured, without philosophical proofs of the soul's immateriality; since it is evident, that he, who made us at first begin to subsist here, sensible, intelligent beings, and for several years continued us in such a state, can and will restore us to the like state in another world, and make us capable there to receive the retribution he has designed to men, according to their doings in this life; and therefore it is not of such mighty necessity to determine one way or the other, as some over zealous for or against the immateriality of the soul have been forward to make the world believe." These are Mr. Locke's words; and I appeal to all unbiased men, whether he does not better secure the belief of a future state, by establishing it on such grounds, as give an equal assurance of it, whether the soul is immaterial, or no; than those, who take pains to persuade men, that a future state is less certain, if the soul is not immaterial.

But besides the uncertainty and danger of this argument, which I have before taken notice of, the usefullness of it, to the generality of mankind, sufficiently shows, that it cannot be the foundation of the belief of a future state. That it is not so to the eastern pagans at this day, we have the evidence of a judicious author, both from the information of the missionaries, who have been longest among them, and his own conversation with them, who tell us, that they believe the *immortality* of the soul, but have no notion of its *immateriality;* and that they only suppose it of a *matter* subtle enough to escape being seen or handled. And that many of the old philosophers, who expected a future state, had no thoughts of the soul's being *immaterial,* anyone must observe, who has read them with attention. And I believe, if well examined, it will appear, that those among them, who had a notion of the soul's being immaterial, did not believe its immortality upon that foundation, but only sought an explication, how the soul by its own nature might be capable of that immortality; which they found great reason to hope for, on other grounds much more firm and persuasive.

But what is yet more considerable, were this proof of the soul's immortality as certain and as universally received, as any self-evident proposition, it would not at all serve to the chief end of our assurance of the soul's immortality, viz. The expectation of rewards and punishments in a future state according to our doings in this life; without which 'tis no matter, whether we think the soul immortal or no. And this we could never have by the most attentive consideration, and the clearest knowledge of what kind of substance the soul is. It must be established on far different grounds, such as the consideration of ourselves as rational and free creatures, of which we have an intuitive, infallible perception; and of an omnipotent being, from whom we are, and on whom we depend, of which we have a demonstrative knowledge within everyone's understanding to whom it is proposed. And if the consequences drawn from them are not sufficient to assure men of a future state of rewards and punishments, as the clearest proofs of the soul's immortality can signify nothing without them, so neither can they add any force to them, and therefore are of no use to the great ends of morality and religion. For suppose to convince an intelligent heathen, who thought the soul material, and doubted of a future state of rewards and punishments, arguments were used to prove the soul in its own nature undissolvable, and that therefore it must remain after death; he might then reasonably enquire in what state it remains, how he may be sure, that it is in a state of rewards and punishments, and that it does not return to the universal soul, of which it may be an effluence; or inform the next parcel of matter it finds fitted for it, as some philosophers have thought. This, it is plain, must be still in doubt to him, notwithstanding those proofs of the soul's immortality; and arguments of another nature must be used to satisfy him in this point, whatever may be most proper to work on his understanding. Suppose those I have before hinted at; That 'tis reasonable to think that the *wise* and *just* Author of our being, having made us capable of *happiness* and *misery,* and given us faculties of discerning and choosing *good or evil,* designed we should be accountable for our actions, and *happy* or *miserable,* according as they are conformable, or not, to that law, which he has established in our very natures, that his will might be certainly known to us; and since it is visibly not so, in the ordinary course of his providence, but all things happen alike to the righteous and the wicked, in this world, 'tis most consonant to reason to think this is only a state of probation, and that the dispensation of rewards and punishments is reserved for a future life; there being no other way to reconcile the partial distribution of things here to that order which we know is agreeable to the divine will, by the conformity it has to our reason, which is a ray of his own wisdom. We will suppose the heathen convinced by these arguments, or others to the same purpose; that he owns it is highly reasonable to conclude there must be a future state of rewards and punishments; but he does not so well digest the soul's being immaterial; he has no notion of a substance without any extension. Suppose then the Remarker should tell him, as he does Mr. Locke, if the soul is not *immaterial*, there can be no certain proof that it is immortal. And I desire him to take this dilemma for the heathen's answer: Either the arguments, by which I have been convinced, that there will be punishments and rewards in a future state, are proofs of it, or they are not; if not, then though the soul should be immortal, I have no assurance that it will be in a state of rewards or punishments; and if they are proofs of a future state, then a future state is equally certain, though the soul be not immaterial, since that does not make it less consonant to the justice and wisdom of God, nor less within his power. I believe the Remarker will find he has no way to solve this dilemma, but must either give up the certainty of rewards and punishments, or the necessity of thinking the soul is immaterial, to prove a future state; and I defy him to establish the belief of rewards and punishments in a future state on any arguments, that will not be equally conclusive, whether the soul is immaterial or not.

This then is evident, that Mr. Locke's supposition, that God may have given (for anything we know) to some systems of matter a power to perceive, and think; does not at all weaken any proof of the soul's immortality, that can be of use to the great ends of religion, for which alone we are concerned to know, that the soul is immortal. And perhaps the insignificance, as to those ends, of our knowing what kind of substance the soul is, may be the reason we are left so much in the dark about it. Our wise maker has proportioned our faculties only to our necessities, and has made his will known to us by a light of nature clear enough to render anyone inexcusable who does not follow it; though the full assurance of an eternal retribution is only given us by Jesus Christ, who has brought life, and immortality, to light, through the Gospel, which I have already shown, that Mr. Locke's principles give us a sure foundation for, both of natural and revealed religion.

Lady Mary Shepherd

LADY MARY SHEPHERD's life has not been very well docu-
mented, and there are only a few facts that are readily available.*
She was born Lady Mary Primrose, the second daughter of Neil
Primrose, the third Earl of Rosebery. This places her in Scotland, where a number of the figures with which she concerns
herself, such as Reid, Stewart, and Brown, also lived. She is by no
means limited in her reading, however, to Scottish philosophers.
She married Henry John Shepherd on April 11, 1808, and her
published writings all appear considerably after the date of her
marriage. Henry John Shepherd was the son of the Rt. Hon.
Sir Samuel Shepherd, Lord Chief Baron of the Exchequer in
Scotland, which again suggests a Scottish connection, although
her father-in-law achieved this position in Scotland subsequent
to the marriage. The *Dictionary of National Biography* says, tan-
talizingly, that she was the author of three philosophical
treatises, but other references, such as that in Samuel Allibone's
*A Critical Dictionary of English Literature and British and
American Authors* (1900) or Robert Blakey's *History of the Philosophy of the Mind* (1850) mention only two: *An Essay on the
Relation of Cause and Effect* (1824) and *Essays on the Perception
of an External Universe* (1827). She also got drawn into a public

---

*I am indebted to M. A. Stewart for putting me in possession of some of these facts.
I thank Eileen O'Neill for calling my attention to the work of Mary Shepherd from
which this selection is drawn.

controversy with John Fearn, a retired naval officer turned philosopher. Fearn made available for publication a brief set of criticisms Shepherd wrote on his book *First Lines of the Human Mind*, which was published in a volume called *Parriana*, put together by E. H. Barker in 1829, along with a lengthy reply by Fearn. Shepherd subsequently responded to this reply in an article in *Fraser's Magazine* in 1832. I am unaware of other events in her life, except that she died on January 7, 1847.

The chief target of both of Shepherd's works is Hume, although she does not in either work confine her attention to him exclusively. Her primary motive, however, in both works, is to provide an alternative to what she sees as Hume's skepticism, which she takes to be conducive to atheism. She is especially concerned that Hume's position on causation may undermine important arguments for the existence of God. She appears to equate Hume's identification of the imagination as the source of our knowledge of causation and of external bodies with the claim that events are uncaused and that external bodies do not exist. She seeks to escape Hume's skepticism by showing that we have within our mental powers, specifically our reason, the capacity to arrive at such knowledge. Shepherd is using the term "reason" quite loosely, however. What she makes it her business to show is that it is rational to believe that events have causes, that like causes have like effects, and that our sensations could not be explained unless external bodies existed. Although she explicitly rejects Reid's and Stewart's claim that it is possible to have nonsensory knowledge of the primary qualities of the external cause of our sensations, holding instead that such a cause is unperceived and unknown, she nevertheless maintains that unknown cause exists. Briefly, she argues that our sensations exhibit a variety that is not due to the unchanging nature of our mental faculties and a "readiness to reappear," which can only be accounted for on the assumption of an external cause. Further, we will not be tempted to adopt Hume's skepticism with regard to causation so long as we understand that a cause is not an antecedent but rather the ground of new qualities, so that, as she sees it, "the future is *involved* in the past" (*Essay on Cause and Effect*, p. 143).

In the selection in this volume, Shepherd tries to differentiate her position from that of Berkeley, with whom she is concerned that she might become confused. This is presumably because she sides with Berkeley against Reid and Stewart on the nature of our ideas. She holds that they have ignored what is widely recognized as a truism that *"perceptions* must necessarily be *conscious,* therefore, they are affections of an animated nature" (*Essays on the Perception of an External World,* p. 254). She takes herself to be agreeing with Berkeley that sensations can only exist in a mind perceiving them. She interprets Berkeley, however, as she had interpreted Hume, as having a largely skeptical thesis, in Berkeley's case that nothing exists except ideas and minds. It is this thesis she sets out to refute, in order to put in its place her own claim that sensations or ideas can serve as what she calls algebraic signs to inform us of their unknown causes.

✧ Selections from
Essays on the Perception of an External Universe

ESSAY I

Consideration of the Erroneous Reasoning Contained in Bishop Berkeley's Principles of Human Knowledge

SECTION I

"When several ideas," says Bishop Berkeley (section 1st,) "(imprinted on the senses) are observed to accompany each other, they come to be marked by one name; and so to be reputed as one thing, thus a certain color, taste, smell, figure, and consistence, are accounted one distinct thing, signified by the

Selections from Lady Mary Shepherd, *Essays on the Perception of an External Universe* (London: John Hatchard and Sons, 1827), 195–219.

name of apple; other collection of ideas form a stone, a tree, a book etc." (Section 3rd, p. 25), "For what are objects but the things we perceive by sense? and what do we perceive but our own ideas or sensations? for, (section 5th,) light and colors, heat and cold, extension and figure, in a word, the things we see and feel, what are they but so many sensations, notions, ideas, impressions on the sense? and is it possible to separate even in thought any of these from perception"(Sec. 9, p. 27). "Some make a distinction between primary and secondary qualities; but extension, figure, and motion, are ONLY *ideas* existing in the mind. And an idea can be like nothing but an idea, for neither these nor their archetypes, can exist in an unperceiving substance" (Section 15th). It is impossible, therefore, that any color or extension at all, or sensible quality whatever, should exist in an unthinking subject without the mind, or indeed, that there should be any such thing as an outward object."

Thus far Bishop Berkeley, on *objects* being *only ideas,* or sensations of sensible qualities, and these ideas as comprehending the primary as well as secondary qualities. Many, I conceive, will think, from what I have said in the foregoing pages, that there is no material difference between my doctrine, and his. But a careful investigation of both, will show there is a very considerable one. For although, I agree with him, first, that nothing can be like a *sensation,* or *idea,* or *perception,* but a *sensation, idea,* and *perception;* secondly, that the primary qualities, *after* the impressions they make on the senses, are sensations, or ideas, or perceptions; as well as the secondary ones. Yet I do not agree with him, in stating, that *objects* are nothing but what we perceive by sense, or that a complete enumeration is made of *all* the ideas which constitute an apple, a stone, a tree, or a book; in the summing up of their *sensible qualities.* For I have made it clear, I trust, by the foregoing argument, that *an object perceived* by the mind is a compound being, consisting of a certain collection of sensible qualities, "mixed with an *idea* the *result of reasoning*" of such qualities being formed by a "continually existing outward and independent set of as various and appropriate causes"; therefore that there must be "*an outward object,*" existing as a cause to excite the inward feeling. The logical error, therefore, of Bishop Berkeley on this part of the subject, is an *incomplete definition;* for no definition is good which does not take notice of *all* the ideas, under the term; and in every object of sense which the mind perceives, the knowledge of its *genus,* as a general effect arising from a *general* cause independent of mind, *is mixed with the sensations or ideas resulting from its special qualities affecting the same.* The notion of this *genus* is omitted in Dr. Berkeley's *definition of an* OBJECT, by the limiting words *but* and *only.*

Bishop Berkeley is guilty of an ambiguity, when he speaks "of ideas being *imprinted on the senses,*" "of our perceiving" *(by sense)* "our *own ideas and sensations,*" for he appears to speak of the "*senses* on which objects are imprinted," as if he intended by them those five organs of sense, viz. the eye, the ear, etc. *vulgarly called the senses,* but which, in truth, have no sense or feeling in themselves as independent of mind; but are mechanical instruments; which as powers modify exterior existences, ere they reach the sentient capacity; the which capacity as a general power or feeling becomes modified thereby; for undoubtedly, the senses as organs cannot perceive what the senses as organs are required to form.[1]

When he speaks of "ideas being imprinted on the senses," *the phrase contains* the very doctrine he is controverting.

The *ideas* of colors cannot be imprinted on the *eye;* nor those of sound on the *ear;* nor those of extension on the *touch;* for there are no such IDEAS, until *after* the eye, as an instrument, has been affected by *some sorts of outward objects,* fitted to convey to the sentient principle, a sensation of color, and so of the rest. Therefore the objects *perceived* by the organs of sense cannot be our ideas, and sensations. Indeed, he does not take notice that he uses the notion of *perception* (which is that upon which the whole argument depends) in two different methods, or meanings. For the term perception, when applied to those objects for whose observation the organs of sense are required, and by which certain qualities are determined upon the perceiving mind, is used as the *notice* the mind takes of the presence of certain qualities *in consequence of the conscious use of the organs of sense,* the use and action of which must, therefore, be in relation to *some* objects which are not the mind; but when applied to the "ideas and sensations of sensible qualities," perception is *only* used as the mental consciousness of those qualities, leaving out the conscious use of the organs of sense, and the ideas of the outward objects which must necessarily have acted on them.

Nor is this reasoning I am using, the mere turning of an expression, for in this sentence "*what are objects* but the things *we perceive by sense*?" and "what do we *perceive* but our ideas and sensations?" there is an offense against one of the plainest and most useful of logical rules; for the argument if placed in a regular syllogism, will be seen to contain a middle term of two different and particular significations from which, therefore, nothing can be concluded.

Let the question be, "Are *objects, ideas* and *sensations* only?" and the middle term, "*The things we perceive,*"—be united with the predicate for the major proposition, and then be altered to—"the things *we perceive by sense*," when joined to the *subject,* for the minor; it will be seen that an inconclusive syllogism is thence formed.—For if the major proposition stands, "Our ideas and sensations, are the only things we perceive," and the minor, "Objects are the things we perceive by sense," the conclusion, viz. "Therefore *objects* are only our ideas and sensations," does not logically follow, because the middle term would then consist of "*two different parts, or kinds,* of the same *universal* idea," i.e. the idea of perception in general; "and this will *never* serve to show whether the subject and predicate agree, or disagree."[2] *For in the general conscious perception of sensible qualities, are included the knowledge that the organs of sense are used, as mechanical instruments acted upon by certain causes, and the* IDEAS *of these causes.* And this conscious use of the mechanical action of the five senses in relation to other beings than the mind, *is a very different part, or kind of the universal idea of perception, from the mental consciousness of* PARTICULAR SENSIBLE QUALITIES *only;* which is also another part, or kind of the general notion of perception; *which general* notion *includes every species of consciousness whatever.* The consciousness whether the organs of sense be used or not, in perceiving objects, is the great criterion of a sane, or insane state of mind, of its waking or sleeping condition; the consciousness that the organs of sense are used, makes all the difference between objects of sense, or objects of memory, reason, or imagination. *By the quick and practical use of the senses subsequent to infancy, the associations of ideas, resulting from reason and experience, are so interwoven and so immediate with the consciousness of their use, that they ought always to be considered as forming a component part of the whole ideas which lie under the terms,* THE OBJECTS OF SENSE. The *objects of sense,* therefore, (under the conscious use of the organs of sense,) are known, (according to the reasoning used in the foregoing chapters of this essay,) to be the *continued, exterior,* and *independent existences* of external nature, exciting ideas, and determining sensations in the mind of a sentient being; but not ONLY to be *ideas* and *sensations.*

In the sentence already commented on, and which contains the sum of Dr. Berkeley's doctrine—the word *object,* as well as the phrase *"perception by sense,"* is of ambiguous application;—for in his use of the word *object,* he begs the question; meaning thereby a collection of sensible qualities, formed by the senses and apprehended by the mind; whereas the adversary means by that word, a set of qualities exterior to the mind, and to which the organs of sense are in relation as mechanical instruments, and of which they take notice as those permanent existences, which the understanding is aware *must needs continue* when unperceived, ere they are transformed by their action into other beings. Objects before the notice of the senses, are not the same things as after their acquaintance with them. All men mean by objects the things which exist previously to their mixture with the action of the organs of sense, and which FROM POWERFUL ASSOCIATION, *they conceive to exist under the forms of their sensible qualities;*—therefore by feigning the contrary notion there can arise no convincing argument.

To go on, however, with the argument, (by which I would show that objects of sense are not *only* the ideas of their sensible qualities,) I observe that reason discovering these objects to be in their relation to each other, as *various* as the *impressions* they convey; also perceives them to be in *one* respect *like* the ideas they create; i.e. in the same proportions and bearings to each other, *outwardly* as they are inwardly. Therefore among the observations we have of "our ideas and sensations" of sensible qualities, we do perceive *something else* than these mere "*ideas* or *sensations*"; for we perceive by *reason*, that those things which must needs be present in order as *causes* to affect the sense, may on account of *their variety*, their *similar distinctness*, and *proportions*, be named, (when considered as existing exterior to the instruments of sense,) by the names they bear when inwardly taken notice of.

Now I consider the observation of this latter circumstance as containing a full answer to all the puzzling contradictions of Bishop Berkeley's theory; for although, in a popular manner, men consider things are *outwardly* the *counterpart* of what they perceive *inwardly;* yet this is not the whole reason of the difference they make amidst things: for the soul does truly in a sense *perceive* outward things, *as* they are when existing outwardly, for after *reason* shows that the qualities of things, in a state of *perception,* cannot *be like* them out of a state of perception, yet being conscious that sensation is only a *simple* act, (a power, a quality,) *it perceives* by the understanding that the *varieties* of things are in relation to each other *outwardly* in the *same proportion* as are the inward sensations. Thus hard and soft, bitter and sweet, heat and cold, round and square, are therefore *perceived* not ONLY to be sensations, but to be certain unknown qualities of objects independent of the mind in *relation to each other,* and in that *state "to continue to exist, ready to appear to the senses when called for."* Popularly, the *sensations these excite, are associated with the notions of the outward objects,* and all their varieties. But when philosophy breaks up this association, she should not take away *more* than what this natural junction of thought has created; Bishop Berkeley does not merely separate what is mixed, but would destroy the whole compound together. This observation, in my opinion, contains a *demonstration* against the Berkelean theory, and restores nature entirely to her rights again. "Equals taken *from equals* the *remainders are equal."* Take *sensation,* simple sensation, the power or capacity of feeling merely, from extension, from color, from sound, and from taste; from heat and cold; from electricity or attraction; from fire, air, water, or earth; from the *perception* of life, or the *idea* of death; from motion or rest. Is there nothing left? Everything is left that has any variety or difference in it. "What are objects" (says Bishop Berkeley) "but the ideas perceived by sense?" They are beings perceived by reason, to be continually, independently, outwardly existing, of the same proportions as are the inward sensations of which they are the effects. Had Bishop Berkeley allowed of the force of a most finished piece of reasoning he uses in respect to the proof of the existence of *other minds* than our own, in behalf also of objects that are not minds, he had not set before the public, some paradoxes, unhappily considered as *unanswerable*. In (sect. 195), he says, "From what has been said, it is plain that we cannot know the existence of other spirits otherwise than by their operations, or the ideas by them excited in us. I perceive several motions, changes, and combinations of ideas, that inform me there are certain particular agents *like myself*, which accompany them and concur in their production. Hence the knowledge I have of *other spirits* is not immediate as is the knowledge of my ideas, but depending on the intervention of ideas, by me referred to agents or spirits *distinct* from myself, as effects or concomitant signs."

Now my argument (however ill I may have executed it) intends the whole way to show "that our knowledge of other objects" (of any kind) is not *immediate* as is the knowledge of our ideas," but depends "on the *intervention* of our ideas," by us referred to "agents or spirits," (to *unknown proportionate causes* distinct from ourselves,) and that the several "*motions, changes,* and *combinations* of ideas, which we perceive, inform us that there are certain particular agents *like ourselves*" (*always* like ourselves as continuing to *exist,* and *in other qualities, plus* or *minus* ourselves) "which accompany them, and concur in their production."

In order, however, to carry the argument a little farther on these matters, let us examine with a greater nicety than we have yet done this proposition;—"figure, extension, and motion are *only* ideas in the perceiving mind,"—and let us select one quality, say *figure,* for this examination, in order to simplify the analysis; then the argument which applies to figure, will also apply to the other qualities.

Let the question be; Is figure an *idea only* in the perceiving mind? Now undoubtedly the sense, inward perception, or notion of figure, (or by whatever word shall be designated the conscious sensation of a living being which it has, under impression of figure,) can *only* be in a perceiving mind; and nothing else can be like it but such another sensation: but this *sense of figure*, is not what the word figure, only means when applied to an object which affects either the sense of sight or touch. It is then a relative term—a sign of a compound notion, signifying a particular sensation *caused* by a particular *cause*, which cause is not a sensation. Moreover, the word *is also understood to be applicable to the proportion which that cause (or "outward continuous object") bears to the other outward beings surrounding it;* (and this without supposing they are the least like our ideas;) for let us consider a round figure, for instance, apart from our perception of it; the *line* which bounds this solid substance *outwardly*, (whatever *line* and *solid* may be,) and parts it from the surrounding atmosphere, (whatever *parting* or *atmosphere* may be,) must still be a *variety*, or *change*, or *difference*, among these outward things, and this difference among outward unknown things, *not like sensations*, is *outward*, and is always meant in that sense by the word, which signifies, *a certain state of continuous existence*, which is independent of mind. The word and notion are *compound*, and each stands for the *cause and effect united*, and not *only* for the *effect*. Philosophers, therefore, ought to be capable of perceiving that figure, extension, and motion, etc. are *not only ideas in the mind*, but are capacities, qualities, beings in nature in relation to each other when exterior to mind.

It is owing to our ideas being the counterparts of the *proportions* of those things, which our reason teaches us must be independent of mind, that Dr. Reid talks of an *intuitive* conception and knowledge of the nature of outward extension, etc. Whereas it is by observing the relations of our ideas which are effects, whose causes must be equal to them, that we have a knowledge of that relation which the independent and permanent objects of the universe must needs bear to each other; if *instinct* only guided us, there would be no more proof of the external world than of a dream, where there is an equal instinct in behalf of what is afterwards acknowledged to be nonexistent.

But the perceptions of the relations which our ideas and sensations bear to each other, and the results therein deduced, put the proof of an external and continually existent universe upon the same footing as the existence of the sensations themselves, and form a deduction as demonstrable, and clear, and convincing as any mathematical certainty whatever.

To go on, Bishop Berkeley however allows *that there are causes* for the sensations of sensible qualities; independent of the perceiving mind. But it is in descanting upon their nature that he is again guilty of as fallacious, and inconclusive, and paradoxical reasoning as that which we have just examined; for he uses the very argument of his adversary, (which he has been industriously endeavouring to destroy,) as an instrument to prove his own doctrine, and I shall now proceed to show that he does so.

SECTION II

(Section 25th and 26th.) "We perceive," says Bishop Berkeley, "a continual succession of ideas; there is therefore *some cause* of these ideas. This *cause* cannot be any quality or idea; for an idea" (section 25th) is an *inert* being, and cannot be the *cause* of any thing. It must therefore be a substance," (section 26th) "and as it has been shown there is no *material* substance, it remains the cause of our ideas, is an incorporeal, active substance or spirit" (section 27th). "A spirit is one simple, undivided, active being, which hath understanding and will" (section 28th). "My own will excites in my mind ideas at pleasure, and by the same power they are destroyed. This making and unmaking of ideas, very properly denominates the mind active" (section 29th). "But the ideas imprinted on sense are not the creatures of my will, there is therefore some other will or spirit which produces them" (section 30th). "Now there are set rules, or established methods, whereby the mind we depend on excites in us the ideas of sense, and these are called the Laws of Nature" (section 156th).[3] "By nature is meant the visible series of effects or sensations imprinted on our mind." The conclusion of the whole matter is, that there is nothing but two sets of objects, viz. "spirits" and "ideas"; "spirits as causes, and ideas as their effects." Now it is plain we can know no more of *activity, indivisibility,* and *simplicity,* as applied to *substance,* called mind, than of *inertness, divisibility,* etc. applied to another sort of substance, called *matter.* These are still only ideas gained in the usual way, rejected when applied to objects of *sense* existing *without the mind,* but made use of by him, when applied to *spirit, existing without the mind.* "Motion" (Bishop Berkeley distinctly says) "is *only an idea* existing in the mind." If so, I ask, what does he know about *activity,* as *absolutely necessary to constitute a* CAUSE, and which CAUSE, he says, *cannot be an* IDEA? because ideas are "visibly *in*active." Also, what notion can he have of cause at all, if he knows of *"nothing but ideas";* and *ideas are not causes,* and what too are the *rules* and *methods* of the working of a spirit, which as rules and methods and laws of nature, cannot themselves be spirit or substance, yet are not allowed to be material beings? And how can the will at pleasure, call upon an idea, when before it begins to call, it must know what it wishes to call, and so must have consciousness of the idea in question, which as an object associated with another idea, can and does truly act as a cause in order to introduce it. But *I* argue as we can distinguish between the capacity for sensation in general, and that for the exciting causes of extension and other qualities in particular, so we have a right to name *this mind,* and *that* body, and that after all the talk of *materialists,* who say, "matter cannot act on mind," ("they are discordant *beings;* so *all* is matter"); And the immaterialists who say the same things, ("and that *all* is mind," for the same reason); it appears perfectly easy that such causes and capacities, such collections of qualities should intermix, and produce those results, which take place under different forms of sensible objects; and which in my opinion are combined by the junction of the qualities of matter, or unknown powers, or qualities in nature; the senses, or instruments fitted to act along with these; and the *mind,* or *sentient principle* and capacity. Nature in her whole works bears witness such is the case.—Also by keeping strictly in view, that the power of sensation is *one* and *simple*—and that subtracting it from all the objects with which we are acquainted, the remaining qualities will bear still to be considered as worthy of holding the various names affixed to their appearances upon the sense, and reasoned on as before;—there will be cause and effect, extension and space; time and eternity; variety of figure and color; heat and cold, merit and demerit; beauty and deformity, etc., etc.

The proportions of all these beings among themselves, the external independent qualities in nature among themselves, corresponding to our perceptions, must be as *various* as they appear to the mind; therefore, there is figure, extension, color, and all qualities whatever. Nor is it necessary in order to support the idea of deity, and his constant presence and providence, to have recourse to the ridiculous notion of his *activity* as a "spirit" upon our senses in order to change our ideas; for whilst the *perception* of sensible qualities *immediately* informs us of our own *sensations,* reason by the intervention of the ideas of their different relations, equally discovers to us insentient existences, as well as that of our own, and other minds; whilst with respect to the being of God, his essential existence, his continued existence, is demonstrated, by the abstract argument used in this treatise. "Whatever variety and changes of being there are, all changes must finally be pushed back to that essence, who *began not to be,* and in whom all dependent beings originally resided, and were first put forth as out-goings of himself in all those varieties of attitudes, wherewith his wisdom and benevolence are able to fit out every variety and gradation of creature."

Notes

1. Dr. Reid on visible figure, etc. is guilty of a like error.

2. Watts's *Logic.*

3. The remaining sections are taken up in answering objections, and are quite immaterial to the subject of these remarks.

Bibliography

General Works

Linda McAlister (editor), *Hypatia's Daughters: 1500 Years of Women Philosophers*. Bloomington: Indiana University Press, forthcoming.

Eileen O'Neill (editor), *Women Philosophers of the Seventeenth and Eighteenth Centuries: A Collection of Primary Sources*. Oxford: Oxford University Press, forthcoming.

Myra Reynolds, *The Learned Lady in England, 1630–1760*. Boston: Houghton Mifflin, 1920.

Hilda Smith, *Reason's Disciples: Seventeenth Century English Feminists*. Urbana: University of Illinois Press, 1982.

Mary Ellen Waithe (editor), *A History of Women Philosophers*, vol. III. Dordrecht: Kluwer Academic Publishers, 1991.

Chapter 1: Princess Elisabeth of Bohemia

WORKS

The correspondence with Descartes is reprinted in: John J. Blom (translator), *Descartes: His Moral Philosophy and Psychology*. New York: New York University Press, 1978.

BIOGRAPHY

Elizabeth Godfrey (Jessie Bedford), *A Sister of Prince Rupert. Elizabeth Princess Palatine and Abbess of Herford*. London: John Lane The Bodley Head, 1909.

SELECTED COMMENTARY

Bernice Zedler, "The Three Princesses" *Hypatia,* Special Issue, The History of Women, vol. 4, no. 1 (Spring 1989), pp. 28–63.

Ruth Mattern, "Descartes's Correspondence with Elizabeth: Concerning the Union and Distinction of Mind and Body." In *Descartes: Critical and Interpretive Essays,* edited by Michael Hooker. Baltimore: Johns Hopkins University Press, 1978, pp. 212–222.

R. C. Richardson, "The 'Scandal' of Cartesian Interactionism" *Mind,* vol. XCI, 1982, pp. 20–37.

Daniel Garber, "Understanding Interaction: What Descartes Should Have Told Elizabeth." *Southern Journal of Philosophy,* 21, Supplement, 1983, pp. 15–32.

Margaret D. Wilson, "Descartes on the Origins of Sensation" *Philosophical Topics,* vol. 19, no 1. (Spring 1991), pp. 293–323.

Chapter 2: Margaret Cavendish, Duchess of Newcastle

WORKS

Poems and Fancies, 1653.
Philosophical Fancies, 1653.
The World's Olio, 1655.
Philosophical and Physical Opinions, 1655.
　　Reissued as *Grounds of Natural Philosophy,* 1668.
Nature's Pictures, 1656.
Plays, 1662.
Orations of Divers Sorts, 1662.
CCXI Sociable Letters, 1664.
Philosophical Letters, 1664.
Observations upon Experimental Philosophy. To which is added, the Description of a New World called The Blazing World, 1666.
The Life of . . . William Cavendish, 1668.
Plays, never before Printed, 1668.

There are no modern editions of Cavendish's philosophical work.

BIOGRAPHY

Douglas Grant, *Margaret the First.* London: Rupert Hart-Davis, 1957.

SELECTED COMMENTARY

Lisa T. Sarasohn, "A Science Turned Upside Down: Feminism and the Natural Philosophy of Margaret Cavendish." *Huntington Library Quarterly,* 47, 1984, pp. 299–307.

Londa Schiebinger, "Margaret Cavendish, Duchess of Newcastle." In *A History of Women Philosophers,* vol. III, edited by Mary Ellen Waithe. Dordrecht: Kluwer Academic Publishers, 1991, pp. 1–20.

Chapter 3: Anne Viscountess Conway

WORKS

The Principles of the Most Ancient and Modern Philosophy, London, 1692; modern edition, edited by Peter Loptson. The Hague: Martinus Nijhoff, 1982.

BIOGRAPHY

Marjorie Hope Nicolson (editor), *The Conway Letters.* Revised edition edited by Sarah Hutton. Oxford: Clarendon Press, 1992.

SELECTED COMMENTARY

Carolyn Merchant, "The Vitalism of Anne Conway: Its Impact on Leibniz's Conception of the Monad." *Journal of the History of Philosophy,* 27 (3) 1979, pp. 255–270.

Jane Duran, "Anne Viscountess Conway: A Seventeenth Century Rationalist." *Hypatia,* 4 (1) (Spring 1989), pp. 64–79.

Lois Frankel, "Anne Finch, Viscountess Conway." In *A History of Women Philosophers,* vol. III, edited by Mary Ellen Waithe. Dordrecht: Kluwer Academic Publishers, 1991, pp. 41–58.

Lois Frankel, "The Value of Harmony." In *Causation in Early Modern Philosophy: Cartesianism, Occasionalism and Preestablished Harmony,* edited by Steven Nadler. University Park: Pennsylvania State University Press, 1993, pp. 197–216.

Richard H. Popkin, "The Spiritualistic Cosmologies of Henry More and Anne Conway." In *Henry More (1614–1687) Tercen-*

tenary Studies, edited by Sarah Hutton. Dordrecht: Kluwer Academic Publishers, 1990, pp. 97–114.

Stuart Brown, "Leibniz and More's Cabalistic Circle." In *Henry More (1614–1687) Tercentenary Studies,* edited by Sarah Hutton. Dordrecht: Kluwer Academic Publishers, 1990, pp. 77–95.

Chapter 4: Damaris Cudworth, Lady Masham

WORKS

E. S. de Beer (editor), Letters to Locke. In *The Correspondence of John Locke,* vols. II and III. Oxford: Clarendon Press, 1976.

A Discourse Concerning the Love of God, London, 1696.

Occasional Thoughts in Reference to a Virtuous or Christian Life, London, 1705.

C. I. Gerhardt (editor), Letters to Leibniz. In *Die Philosophischen Schriften von Leibniz,* vol. 3. Berlin: 1975–90.

BIOGRAPHY

None, but for an account of Masham's relationship to Locke, see Sheryl O'Donnell, " 'My Idea in your Mind': John Locke and Damaris Cudworth Masham." In *Mothering the Mind,* edited by Ruth Perry and Martine Watson Brownley. New York: Holmes and Meier, 1984, pp. 26–46.

SELECTED COMMENTARY

Lois Frankel, "Damaris Cudworth Masham: A Seventeenth Century Feminist Philosopher." *Hypatia,* vol. 4, no. 1 (Spring 1989), pp. 80–90.

Sarah Hutton, "Damaris Cudworth, Lady Masham: between Platonism and Enlightenment." *The British Journal for the History of Philosophy,* vol. 1, no. 1 (Spring 1993), pp. 29–54.

Chapter 5: Mary Astell

WORKS

A Serious Proposal to the Ladies, for the Advancement of Their True and Greatest Interest, by a Lover of her Sex, 1694.

A Serious Proposal to the Ladies, Part II: wherein a method is offer'd for the improvement of their minds, 1697.

Some Reflections upon Marriage, Occasion'd by the Duke and Dutchess of Mazarine's Case; which is also consider'd, 1700.

Letters Concerning the Love of God between the Author of the Proposal to the Ladies and Mr. John Norris, wherein his Discourse shewing That it ought to be entire and exclusive of all other Loves is further cleared and justified, 1695.

Moderation Truly Stated: Or a Review of a Late Pamphlet entitl'd Moderation a Vertue with a Prefatory Discourse to Dr. D'Avenant concerning his late Essays on Peace and War, 1704.

A Fair Way with the Dissenters and their Patrons. Not writ by Mr. L---y, or any other Furious Jacobite whether Clergyman or Layman; but by a very moderate person and dutiful subject to the Queen, 1704.

An Impartial Enquiry into the Causes of Rebellion and Civil War in this Kingdom. In an examination of Dr. Kennett's Sermon Jan. 31, 1703–4 and Vindication of the Royal Martyr, 1704.

The Christian Religion as Profess'd by a Daughter of the Church of England, 1705.

Bartelmy Fair or an Enquiry after Wit in which due Respect is had to a Letter concerning Enthusiasm. To my Lord XXX by Mr. Wotton, 1709.

Modern edition. Bridget Hill (editor and introducer), *The First English Feminist: Reflections Upon Marriage and other writings by Mary Astell.* New York: St. Martin's Press, 1986.

BIOGRAPHY

Ruth Perry, *The Celebrated Mary Astell: An Early English Feminist.* Chicago: University of Chicago Press, 1986.

SELECTED COMMENTARY

Joan Kinnaird, "Mary Astell and the Conservative Contribution of English Feminism." *Journal of British Studies*, vol. XIX, no. 1 (Fall 1979), pp. 53–75.

Kathleen M. Squadrito, "Mary Astell's Critique of Locke's View of Thinking Matter." *Journal of the History of Philosophy*, vol. XXV, no. 3 (July 1987), pp. 433–439.

Kathleen M. Squadrito, "Mary Astell." In *A History of Women Philosophers*, vol. III, edited by Mary Ellen Waithe. Dordrecht: Kluwer Academic Publishers, 1991, pp. 87–99.

Margaret Atherton, "Cartesian Reason and Gendered Reason." In *A Mind of Her Own*, edited by Louise Antony and Charlotte Witt. Boulder: Westview Press, 1992.

Chapter 6: Catharine Trotter Cockburn

WORKS

The Works of Mrs. Catharine Cockburn, Theological, Moral, Dramatic, and Poetical, several of them now first printed, revised and published with an account of the life of the author by Thomas Birch. 2 vols. London: J. and P. Knapton, 1751.

> Includes: *A Discourse concerning a Guide in Controversies*, 1707; *A Defense of Mr. Locke's Essay of Human Understanding*, 1702; *A Letter to Dr. Holdsworth*, 1726; *A Vindication of Mr. Locke's Christian Principles, from the injurious Imputations of Dr. Holdsworth; Remarks upon some Writers in the Controversy concerning the Foundation of Moral Virtue and Moral Obligation. With some thoughts concerning Necessary Existence; the Reality and Infinity of Space; the Extension and Place of Spirits; and on Dr. Watts's Notion of Substance*, 1743; *Remarks upon the Principles and Reasonings of Dr. Rutherforth's Essay on the Nature and Obligations of Virtue; in Vindication of the contrary Principles and Reasonings inforced in the Writings of the late Dr. Samual Clarke*, 1747.

BIOGRAPHY

Life, by Thomas Birch, included in the collected *Works of Mrs. Catharine Cockburn*.

SELECTED COMMENTARY

Mary Ellen Waithe, "Catharine Trotter Cockburn." In *A History of Women Philosophers*, vol. III, edited by Mary Ellen Waithe. Dordrecht: Kluwer Academic Publishers, 1991, pp. 101–125.

Martha Brandt Bolton, "Some Aspects of the Philosophy of Catharine Trotter." *Journal of the History of Philosophy*, vol. XXXI, no. 4 (October, 1993), pp. 565–588.

Chapter 7: Lady Mary Shepherd

WORKS

An Essay upon the Relation of Cause and Effect, controverting the Doctrine of Mr. Hume, concerning the Nature of that Relation; with Observations upon the Opinions of Dr. Brown and Mr. Lawrence, connected with the same subject. London: Printed for T. Hookham, Old Bond Street, 1824.

Essays on the Perception of an External Universe and other Subjects Connected with the Doctrine of Causation. London: John Hatchard and Sons, 1827.

"Observations of Lady Mary Shepherd on the 'First Lines of the Human Mind.'" In *Parriana: or Notices of the Rev. Samuel Parr, LL. D.*, collected from various sources, printed and manuscript and in part written by E. H. Barker, esq. London: Henry Colburn, New Burlington Street, 1828, pp. 624–627.

"Lady Mary Shepherd's Metaphysics." *Fraser's Magazine for Town and Country*, vol. V, no. XXX (July 1832), pp. 697–708.

BIOGRAPHY

None.

SELECTED COMMENTARY

None.